Dancing for God After Fifty

Pastor P.K. Roberts

Published by
International Soaring Eagles Press
Selfridge, Michigan

Inquiries should be addressed to:
Pastor P.K. Roberts
International Soaring Eagles Ministries
Post Office Box 46516
Mount Clemens, Michigan 48046
(586) 468-4213

CONTENTS

Acknowledgments

First and foremost, I praise God for the wonderful journey of life and ministry. There are many to whom I give thanks for assisting me along this journey of life. My parents, the late Jocephus and Vessie Lee Fleming, loved and supported me as I struggled to thrive and become in the state of Mississippi. They taught me to praise and worship God through all things—the good and bad. My mama was a dancer. Her song through the rough days was, "We'll Understand It Better Bye and Bye." She was so right. As I have matured life has taken on a new meaning. Even my understanding of dance, praise and worship has changed.

There are too many people who have contributed to this work directly or indirectly to express my appreciation to each one individually. However, I must thank the Selfridge Chapel Family for allowing their pastor to practice on them. They were my very first audience. Julia and Audrey, you will never know how much your smiles and words of encouragement motivated me to continue. Marcia, your Monday morning critiques always provided the fuel to try again the next Sunday. Michelle and Alex, you two know how to make a Unit Ministry Team function in peace and love. This congregation provided the support that a fledgling dancing pastor needed to empower her to say "YES" to the call of God. Thanks.

LaSonya Thomas, The Ministry in Motion from New Testament Church of God in Christ, Detroit, Michigan, Minister Leya Elijah-Oliver, The World Shaker's Outreach and the Faith, Hope and Love Christian Center, Muskegon, Michigan, you embraced, encouraged and allowed me to dance when I did not know that I could dance. Thank you so much for including me when I needed it most.

Karen, Dixie, and Shannon, without your assistance I could have never met the deadline for this book. Thanks a million for your kind push to finish this project. You kept me focused; therefore, burning midnight oil and attending early morning 5 a.m. prayer sessions really paid off. I know that God has something else for us to do in the near future.

Prayer/Praise is the foundation of what I do and who I am. The prayer warriors Stephanie Jackson, Carol Fuller, Jeannie Johnson and Bonita Jewett assisted in birthing this book. My humble thanks. Reverend Sir Walter and Sandra Scott, Dr. Steven and Paulette Jordan, Reverend James and Miriam Cooper, you have prayed, encouraged and pushed me out of the nest. Thanks for insisting that I SOAR!

Michelle West, Ted and Chandra Lewis and Keith Smith, you taught me the importance of an Armor Bearer. Thanks a million for holding up my arms. This battle is won and now we must prepare for others to come.

My deepest gratitude goes to my long-suffering husband, who is my greatest supporter and fan. David, your love, encouragement and support granted me the framework to flourish. Thanks for praising God with me through the ups and downs of this journey. Eddie and Davola, even though you are not home, your calls and support always lift me up. Verletta and Arnel, you are the added wind beneath my wings. Thanks for being the children you are to me.

Finally, I thank God for using my frail humanity to bring a word that is designed to bring Him praise.

Acknowledgments

This book is to "Your Glory" and in obedience to Your command. Now I pray that You breath upon my inferior work and usher a blessing into the lives of every reader.

Foreword

Let them praise His name in the dance.
(Psalm 149:3 KJV)

This simple command has affected so many for so long and the church has still not seen the fullness of God in this area. Yet, this is the most awesome time to be alive in the Church as we see Dance and the Arts come into their fullness and completeness as the people of God press into this area of worshipping their God. In this book, Pastor Roberts provides a road map with fresh vision and inspiration to move forward on the journey to using Dance as a tool of worship, a weapon of war and a cry for intimacy with God.

Sometimes God will allow circumstances into our lives to bring us to this place of intimacy. There was a season in my life where I had gone through a very difficult time and had not danced before the Lord or ministered in dance for several months. I can recall one day in prayer where I was so devastated, discouraged and felt that I could never dance again. God spoke to me and said, "Get up and dance before me even if it's a sacrifice and I will heal you and set you free." Slowly I began to move and felt like every bone in my body weighed a ton. The more I danced the more I began to flow and the more I felt the presence of the Lord. Truly it was all about Him and how He was using and would continue to use me.

In all my years of training in the area of dance, there was always instruction and practicum. Hours were spent studying the body and training the body to do what at times I never thought it could accomplish. The key to it all was the fact that I was preparing my body to be used of God. I didn't know until many years later that it was all about Him and not about me. God prepared my body and through the years prepared my spirit and soul to know Him. He never allowed me to dance for secular audiences. I didn't understand then but know now the importance of being set apart for my Savior. Again, it wasn't about me but all about Him. All of the preparation allowed me to bring the beauty of the Dance and knowing Him to many who needed healing, restoration, love and a touch from the Father. Similarly, ministry training did the same thing and I came to realize how dance and all the preparation were really about ministry to God and His people. I came to understand that He was my audience of One and as I ministered to Him then He poured out His anointing on His people. I came to realize that what touched people when I danced was the passion I had for God and ministering to Him.

In this book are the many truths that I have experienced and realized through the years of dancing before the Lord. These are truths that everyone involved in the Dance Ministry must hear. Pastor Roberts has left no stone unturned. The amazing thing is that this book has been forged out of revelation, reality and an encounter with God. When we witness the passion that she has experienced, then we desire it for our own lives.

As you read this book, press on and experience an intimacy with God that you have never had. As you do, it will compel you to enter in and Dance before Him. You will never be the same!

Dr. Sherill A. Piscopo
Evangel Association of Churches and Ministries

Chapter 1
Dancing for God After Fifty

Miriam the prophetess, Aaron's sister, took a tambourine, and all the women followed her with tambou-rines, dancing. (Exodus 15:20 MSG)

I told myself I would not go out like this! I was a half-century old and sitting on the sidelines watching others do the very things I once loved doing. I felt old, weighing 253 pounds, hair graying, and experiencing a lack of luster for living. Even leaving my house was a chore. Simple decisions became laborious for me. I could hardly bear to think about what I would wear for the day or how I should style my hair. With the children out of the house, I was now entering a new chapter in my life. My own mother's death caused me to see that this life is no more than a vapor or a fading flower. The joy that once pulled me to the dance floor had vanished. Somewhere along the way I had lost it. Instead of floating like a butterfly and crisscrossing my feet to the tune of life, I was moving in a slow foot-dragging shuffle. This depression placed me in a foreign land, the unfamiliarity of which made my life gloomy and sad. In the face of this heaviness, I resolved that I would not go out like this. I made a solemn vow to myself; I shall live and not die!

When I was growing up in the sticks of Monticello, Mississippi, there were precious few extra-curricular activities available to me. I amused myself on many days by swirling and turning in front of the mirror

11

and creating new dances that I would proudly show off to my friends at school. I loved swaying to the tunes of "Respect" by Aretha Franklin and "Respect Yourself" by Mom and Pop Staples. During a time when segregation was rampant in the South, these songs took on a new meaning for a young teenager in search of true identity and self-respect. Dancing offered another avenue to express the freedom I longed for.

When I received Christ into my life, I changed dance partners from Satan to Jesus and enjoyed a freedom that I never knew existed. The lyrics of my music changed along with my dance steps. So much about my life changed, but my desire to dance did not. I attended church waiting for an opportunity to dance before the Lord. Finally, my opportunity came and I realized that I loved dancing more than ever.

People would let me know how much they were blessed by watching me dance. One elderly gentleman declared, "I have never seen anyone enjoy dancing like you, child. Keep dancing for the Lord because for old folk like me, our dancing days are over." There was a special anointing on moving to songs like "Power in the Blood" or "Nothing but the Blood of Jesus"! I felt victorious when I danced, and these powerful hymns became my dance songs. This was my way of saying, "Thank You, Lord, for saving and changing me!"

During this time, it didn't matter to me how long the service was, just as long as the preacher was anointed and the singers were singing with all their heart. I just wanted to cut a step for the Lord. I was full of energy and on fire for the Lord. This love for God and my desire to make Him smile through my dancing continued until the age of forty-eight, but something happened then and I found myself sitting on the sidelines, waiting for younger women to praise God in dance. For some reason I began to feel like the time had come for me to settle down and act my age. I sat in church with my legs crossed and sometimes I would fold my arms just to hold myself down on the pew. *Let the younger women dance.* I thought. *You have had your turn. It's now time for you to sit.* The self-examination continued. *Do you know of any preacher dancing and sliding over the floor? Sit down and encourage others to dance.*

Slowly, I realized that not only was I not dancing— no one else in my congregation was dancing either.

I had the idea that being the pastor of the church meant I was to exhort *others* to dance. I, as their pastor, was to just lift my hands to the Lord. Finally, one day during a service I attempted to dance and to my amazement, I realized the joy of dancing was gone. Being married, being a mother, having a meaningful career and living in beautiful California did nothing to bring back my joy, but then an event occurred that changed my mind. My husband, Elisha David, and I were born in the same year and we decided to celebrate our 50th birthday together. At our Quinquaginta Celebration, a 10–year-old girl praised God through dance as I had never seen before. She was awesome. Her dancing ignited a fire that simmered in my spirit for two years. A living flame once again blazed within me.

One Sunday before my sermon God spoke to me and said, "I want you to dance for Me."

My reaction was, "What? When? Where? What are you talking about, God?"

During the following week at 5:00 a.m. prayer, God would answer each question. He let me know what to wear, which song to use and guided me so the dance was choreographed to fit my sermon for the Sunday morning worship experience. I must admit. I was a scared sister. I had never danced like this before. This really was a new thing for me.

I called my daughter, Davola, about 3:00 a.m., and she just happened to be up baking cookies for her new husband. Was this just a coincidence? I think not. I told her what was happening with me and asked her, "Do you know of any 50-year-old female preacher, a pastor of a conservative church, dancing at the Sunday morning worship service? How do you think the congregation will receive it? What do you think?"

Davola exclaimed, "Mama, you have never been concerned before about what people think! You should do what you know God is telling you to do! However, I do want to ask if there is someone else who can do this for you?"

That was my question to God, "Is there someone else younger who can do this, Father?"

I was floored when He answered, "You are the one for this season. I am calling you to soar as an eagle during this year of grace. I am doing a *"New Thing"* in you."

"Yes, Lord!" I cried.

The time was at hand for ministry. I had prayed, practiced and prepared for this moment throughout the week. When the time came for me to dance during my sermon, I felt exhilarated. I had not experienced this feeling for many years. No one could have ever convinced me prior to that day that people would be so blessed. The anointing of God was in the house. Members of the congregation actually applauded at the end of the dance.

The following week God implored me to dance again at the annual Easter Sunrise Service to the song "We Shall Behold Him." I had not thought of this song in years. This time I asked two children from my congregation to accompany me.

They were eager to dance for God. Their parents brought them to rehearsal and purchased the outfits and the purple ribbon for our sashes. We only had time for three rehearsals. Resurrection Sunday was upon us. We were clothed in white garments with purple sashes. We looked awesome. As the sun rose over Lake Saint Clair, the backdrop for the service, Jesus arose in the hearts of those watching us dance. I could sense the Presence of God throughout the worship experience. During the dance I knew without a shadow of doubt that God had called me to another dimension in ministry.

About this time, Pastors Oliver and LaVerne Haney, longtime friends, invited me to preach for their morning worship service. Pastor Haney is a renowned homiletician, past Dean of Church of God In Christ Seminary and Interim President of Interdenominational Center in Atlanta, Georgia. This invitation had come months earlier before God had given me my marching orders to dance again. As I prepared for this assignment, the following Scripture dropped into my spirit.

Study to show yourself approved unto God, a worker who needs not be ashamed, and correctly handles the word of truth. (2 Timothy 2:15 NIV)

I did not share with the Haneys prior to service that I planned to dance because I did not know what their reactions would be. I knew they loved our family, and through the years they have offered wise counsel. I knew that if I were to be criticized, they would do it in a loving manner. But I knew above all I needed to be obedient to the call of God. I followed God's instructions. It was tough not to do what I was familiar with when it came to preaching, but the Lord was leading me in a new and fresh way that brought revival to my heart and the hearts of the congregation. I obeyed the Spirit and delivered a message in Sermonic Dance. God blessed my efforts and after worship many people encouraged me by saying, "Your ministry was so refreshing! I will go home and study the life of Miriam." They also asked, "How did you come into Sermonic Dancing? Who taught you this style of ministry?" And then they said, "Will you come and preach and dance for us again?"

The affirmation from my friends, Pastors Oliver and LaVerne Haney, gave me the courage to step out and really soar in this ministry. They embraced the ministry of Sermonic Dance and me so completely that it shocked me. In addition to my surprise, a few key-strokes on the computer revealed information about praise dance, liturgical dance, prophetic dance seminars, workshops, classes and conventions throughout the United States. These teachings have assisted me in perfecting this new-found ministry.

After my Quinquaginta Celebration, a gradual transformation began to take place in me. I had made a solemn vow that I would not go out like this and my Heavenly Father has helped me keep that vow. First, I started losing the extra weight I had been carrying around. The devil wanted me fat so that I couldn't dance for the Lord. He comes to steal, kill and destroy. I now weigh 178 pounds, replacing sizes 18 and 20 with 14 and 16.

Second, medications are totally eliminated from my medicine cabinet. Now I use herbs and food supplement-ation and practice eating properly. My food really is my medicine. I drink Aloe Vera and Mangosteen Herbal Juices every day and eat my share of Omega 3, PhytoDyfense and other healthy supplements. Third, I have employed a personal trainer, not because I could afford her, but because I could not afford to be sick and die prematurely from degenerative diseases of aging. You see, my father died from a heart attack, my mother had a massive stroke, and my grandparents had diabetes and high blood pressure. I refuse to go out like this without a fight. As a result of these major life changes, my blood pressure is 120/80, no diabetes and low cholesterol. I'm looking good and feeling super fantastic!

God has called this fifty-two year old preaching pastor, who has been married for twenty-nine years and is a mother of two adult children, to dance, swirl, whirl, twirl and bow down before Him. To Him I give all glory, honor and praise!

As I looked back over my life I thought of the precious Blood-bought victories God has given me through my dance ministry. I thought of the other women who were where I was at experiencing hopelessness. I wanted to share how God has used this anointed ministry to cause me to triumph in Christ Jesus! The Bible teaches that God is not a respecter of persons. The victory He has given to me, He is willing and able to give to my sisters and brothers-in-Christ. So, I went to prayer and the Lord directed me to write this book. He asked me to share my journey. God has taken my mourning and turned it into dancing.

As God called me into this "New Thing" called "Dance Ministry," my appetite to learn all I could as quickly as possible became insatiable. I read, attended workshops, seminars, conferences, surfed the net, counseled with experts in the field, prayed, practiced and prayed some more. As a result the following pages I offer to you as God has given them to me to share with the Body of Christ.

Praise be to the God and Father of our Lord Jesus Christ, the Father of compassion, and the God of all comfort, who comforts us in all our troubles, so that we can comfort those in any trouble with the comfort we ourselves receive from God. (2 Corinthians 1:3-4 TNIV)

Chapter 2
To Dance or Not to Dance

To dance or not to dance? That seems to be the controversial question in the church today. Be prepared to come in contact with those who object to the ministry of dance. Attempt to keep a Christ-like spirit when you endure criticism. We need to stay sweet and humble and become part of the solution to our critics rather than part of the problem. Almost always when someone disapproves of dancing in the church it's because they may have had a negative past experience. Here are some of the major complaints that I have discovered in my short time in this powerful ministry.

Lack of Modesty

A major complaint is a lack of modesty in costume attire. Some people are offended by "too tight" or "too revealing" costumes. Each dancer being sensitive to the Holy Spirit and dressing modestly for every performance can easily correct this.

Lack of Preparation

Another objection may be that the dancers weren't prepared, danced to substandard choreography or the dance team hadn't practiced enough. Once again, with proper training and preparation this does not have to be an issue. Be sure you are well prepared as you minister for the Lord. Be the best you can be for Jesus!

Relevancy of Scriptures

Another obstacle that a person, pastor or church might overcome in experiencing freedom in dancing before the Lord is to see that this form of worship is in the Bible. They question if it is scriptural or not. Let's look at just a few examples of dancing before the Lord in the Word of God.

Jeremiah prophesied that there will be dancing when Israel is restored.

Again I will build you, and you shall be rebuilt, o virgin of Israel! Again you shall take up your tambourines, and go forth to the dances of the merrymakers. Then the virgin shall rejoice in the dance, and the young men and the old together: for I will turn their mourning into joy and will comfort them, and give them joy for their sorrow. (Jeremiah 31:4,13)

Moses records in the Book of Exodus that Miriam led the women in a victory dance. Miriam was called a prophetess. And it is plain to see that all Israel viewed Miriam's dance as a prophetic gift as the women followed her and joined in with their tambourines, dancing.

Miriam the prophetess, Aaron's sister, took a tambourine, and all the women followed her with tambourines, dancing. (Exodus 15:20 MSG)

Another powerful example from the Word of God is when David danced before the Lord with all his might.

And David was dancing before the Lord with all his might. Then it happened as the ark of the Lord came into the city of David that Michal, the daughter of Saul looked out of the window and saw King David leaping and dancing before the Lord; and she despised him in her heart. (2 Samuel 6:14,16)

We are commanded in Scripture to praise Him in a dance.

Let them praise His name with dancing. Praise Him with timbrel and dancing. (Psalms 149:3, 150:4)

A time to weep and a time to laugh; a time to mourn and a time to dance. (Ecclesiastes 3:4 KJV)

They send forth their little ones like a flock, and their children dance. (Job 21:11 KJV)

Other passages of Scripture that affirm consecrating our bodies for His glory and service are found throughout the Word of God.

I urge you therefore, brethren, by the mercies of God, to present your bodies a living and holy sacrifice, acceptable to God, which is your spiritual service of worship. (Romans 12:1)

Do you not know that your body is a temple of the Holy Spirit who is in you, whom you have from God, and you are not your own? For you have been bought with a price: therefore glorify God in your body. (1 Corinthians 6:19-20)

Ministers of Dance willingly offer their bodies as living sacrifices to the Lord through dance, which is their spiritual service of worship. They have made a conscious decision to glorify God through their bodies being used as an instrument of the Lord.

Your Body is a Temple of the Holy Spirit

Do you not know that your body is the temple—the very sanctuary—of the Holy Spirit Who lives within you, Whom you have received (as a Gift) from God? You are not your own, you were bought for a price—purchased with a preciousness and paid for, made His own. So then, honor God and bring glory to Him in your body. (1 Corinthians 6: 19 AMP)

Your Body is a Dwelling Place for Christ

In Him—and in fellowship with one another—you yourselves also are being built up (into this structure) with the rest, to form a fixed abode (dwelling place) of God in (by, through) the Spirit. (Ephesians 2:22 AMP)

Your Body is a Vessel for Honor

Those who cleanse themselves from the latter will be instruments for noble purposes, made holy, useful to the Master and prepared to do any good work. (2 Timothy 2:21 TNIV)

Your Body is a Container for the Kingdom of God

Nor will people say, "Look! Here (it is)! Or, See, (it is) there!" For behold, the kingdom of God is within you (in your hearts) and among you (surrounding you). (Luke 17:21 AMP)

Your Body Possesses a Precious Treasure

However, we possess this precious treasure (the divine Light of the Gospel) in (frail, human) vessels of earth, that the grandeur and exceeding greatness of the power may be shown to be of God and not from ourselves. (2 Corinthians 4:7 AMP)

As we dig a little deeper in Scripture we can find other confirmations that God loves worshipful dance. In Strong's Concordance we discover Hebrew words for dance or worship. (The reference numbers from Strong's Concordance are in parenthesis.)

Hebrew Words for Dance

ALATS (5970) to jump for joy, rejoice

But let the righteous be glad; let them exult before God; Yes, let them rejoice with gladness. (Psalm 68:3)

CHAGAG (2287) to move in a circle, dance, march in a sacred procession

These things I remember and I pour out my soul within me. For I used to go along with the throng and lead them in procession to the house of God, with the voice of joy and thanksgiving, a multitude keeping festival. (Psalm 42:4)

HALIYKAH (1979) a going, way, traveling company, a march, procession, a walking a caravan or company

They have seen Thy procession, O God, the procession of my God, my King, into the sanctuary. The singers went on, the musicians after them, in the midst of the maidens beating tambourines. (Psalm 68:24-25)

MECHOWLAH (4246) company of dancers

When Jephthah came to his house at Mizpah, behold, his daughter was coming out to meet him with tambourines and with dancing. Now she was his one and only child; besides her he had neither son nor daughter. (Judges 11:34)

23

RAQAD (7540) to stamp, so spring about wildly or to leap for joy, to dance, jump, skip

A time to weep, and a time to laugh; a time to weep, and a time to dance. (Ecclesiastes 3:4)

SCHACAH (7812) to worship, to bow down

And Abraham said to his young men, "Stay here with the donkey, and I and the lad will go yonder; and we will worship and return to you." (Genesis 22:5)

YADA (3034) to revere or worship with extended hands; to use the hand (motion of throwing a stone or arrow); to bemoan by wringing of hands, to cast out, make confession, praise, shout, give thanks, glorify, raising the hands with graceful gestures

I will give thanks to the Lord with all my heart; I will tell of all Thy wonders. I will be glad and exult in Thee; I will sing praise to Thy name, O Most High. (Psalm 9:1-2)

TOWDAH (8426) extension of the hands; adoration; specifically a choir of worshippers; sacrifice of praise of thanks

Those who sacrifice thank offerings honor me, and to the blameless I will show my salvation. (Psalm 50:23 TNIV)

From this simple Bible study we can see that men and women, boys and girls, can all praise Him through dance. God's Word gives every believer the green light to praise Him in this unique way. Let's settle it once and for all in our hearts and minds that it is God's will for His Church to dance before Him!

Chapter 3
Dance Fever

God can take a ministry of dance and make it a living, moving work of visual art. Divine dancing can take place in the privacy of the dancer's home, a church service, a festival, Vacation Bible School, a youth rally, a prayer breakfast, a conference, a parade, a seminar or even a picnic. Spiritual dancing can take place any-where and anytime. This is what happened to me. I had never had a dance lesson or attended a dance seminar or conference when I was called to dance. A dancer may have years of training and experience or God may call someone to a dancing ministry that has no experience at all. God may use one dancer or a whole team of dancers to bring glory to His Name! The dance team may vary in age, sex, size and ability. God is a God of variety and takes delight in using people to help bring deliverance to captive souls. The ways of God seem foolish to humans, but there are many testimonies of men, women, boys and girls telling of how they were completely delivered from a lifetime of bondage when they attended a Holy Ghost meeting where there was great liberty and moving of the Holy Spirit through dance.

Now the Lord is the Spirit; and where the Spirit of the Lord is there is liberty. (2 Corinthians 3:17)

Various Types of Divine Dancing

There are various types of divine dancing. At times they may even seem to overlap when the Holy Spirit is moving. An example would be when the Holy Spirit uses

Intercessory Dance and Prophetic Dance together. Bondages may be broken through Intercessory Dance and the Holy Spirit takes it a step further. The dancer senses victory and then moves into a Prophetic Dance letting the congregation know that God has heard and answered their prayer of intercession. Let's take a few minutes to become better acquainted with the different divine dances.

Intercessory Dance

Dancing before the Lord breaks the chains of the enemy. One precious elderly sister-in-the-Lord shared that her daughter was bent on committing suicide. The dear mother of this hurting child prayed earnestly that God would somehow loose her from this tormenting suicidal spirit. Nothing seemed to be happening and one day this precious mother found her daughter unconscious lying in a pool of blood. Her girl had once again attempted to take her own life. The ambulance came and rushed her off to the emergency room. The doctor came into the emergency waiting room and informed the grieving mother that one of these times her daughter was going to accomplish what she had set out to do. This mother was at Wit's End Corner. She immediately removed herself from the emergency room and found a place where she could talk to her Heavenly Father. She stood on the promises of God for her daughter. Suddenly, a little bit of heaven came to earth as the Lord prompted this mother to dance in faith before Him a dance of intercession. This type of dancing is a spiritual exercise of faith for bleak situations. The dancer is communicating with the Holy Spirit and the Holy Spirit is communicating through the dancer that God is in control. The dancer is expressing various forms of human need to God and sometimes allowing God to reply.

As this dear mother cried out to the Lord and danced before Him, the demonic stronghold in her daughter's life was broken. God spoke and told her that her daughter would live and not die. He also told her that she would live to see her daughter playing her violin for Jesus. A few years later, just as God had shown this mother, her daughter stood on the platform of the church, completely delivered, and played "What a Friend We Have in Jesus" on her violin. The suicidal spirit never returned. This mother stood in the gap for her daughter when it looked as if there was no hope, but through her obedience to God in prayer and Intercessory Dance the victory came.

Lyrical Dance

Another form of divine dancing is called Lyrical Dance. This is a type of spiritual warfare dance. A lone dancer or a team of dancers focus on interpreting the words of strategically selected songs. Some may be trained in dance, while others are not. This dance is done with much confidence and boldness that speak to the congregation's circumstances or to the devil with directness.

A few years ago a praise team of young people performed a Lyrical Dance to Ray Boltz's song, "Watch the Lamb" at a county fair. The atmosphere was not like a church service. The praise team was a little nervous as they looked out in the audience and saw that most of the people there were not believers, but they felt that God had called them to perform this Lyrical Dance at this time. They prayed together to attempt to calm their nerves. The emcee announced that it was their turn to come to the stage and perform. The minute the music started, a holy hush fell over the crowd. The Holy Spirit descended in such a way that people wept as they watched these young people minister through Lyrical Dance. When the performance was over, the young people exited the stage and were met by a group of people expressing to them that they had never had such a moving experience! The Holy Spirit shows up when we allow Him to empty us of ourselves, and then He fills us up with Jesus! One of the young dancers exclaimed,

"We must never put God in a box! He is a God of variety and can use many different techniques to bring others to know Him. Tonight He chose to use Lyrical Dance!"

Liturgical Dance

Liturgical Dance is the art of interpreting sacred music and scripture through motion. It is a dance that brings people closer to God by interpreting familiar music and words in a visual format. Many times a church choir sings "How Great Thou Art" and the congregation is transported to heavenly places in Christ. They recognize immediately that they are standing on holy ground. So it is with Interpretative Liturgical Dance. It adds to the understanding and appreciation of His Presence. Liturgical Dance is an intimate dance between the Lord and the dancer. Movements are personal, reverent, and yielded.

In Liturgical Dance it is as if the dancer knows spiritual sign language. The dancer's movement brings the text to life. As the anointing rests on the dancers, a change takes place. God's holy presence fills the room. God is in the house! Dancers may include flags, banners, tambourines and other worshipping tools.

Celebration Dance

A Celebration Dance is a dance of intense victory. It's full of excitement! The dancers are joyful because God has intervened in a hopeless situation and caused them to triumph. It's a "party" dance that shouts, "God answered my prayers and He will answer your prayers, too!"

Years ago there was a precious mother who had prayed for years for the conversion of her grown son. One day an evangelist came to town and had good old-fashioned revival meetings. The first few nights the mother pleaded with her son to attend. He refused. But on the last night, to the mother's surprise, her son went with her to the service. The minute they walked into the service the mother knew God was up to something. The music was divine. The preaching was powerful. Then, the evangelist opened the altars for the altar call. That mother had her eyes shut tightly and prayed earnestly that her boy would accept Christ. When she finally opened her eyes, she saw that her son was kneeling at the altar weeping. The Holy Ghost fell on that mother and she began to dance and clap her hands in victory. Soon others joined her. All of Heaven was having a celebration, and some precious souls, whose prayers God had answered, joined in the party.

Prophetic Dance

The Holy Spirit is trying to speak to God's people through Prophetic Dance. It can take place during an individual's private prayer time, a seminar setting or a church service. There is no end to how or where the Holy Spirit may use this divine dance. This is a God-given dance that ministers to a person's heart with a specific word of encouragement, direction or confirmation.

During a weekly ladies' prayer meeting, God used all of the women attending in Prophetic Dance. They had been praying for several months for their area to experience revival. They lived in a very "religious" state and longed for Jesus to pass by and bring true repentance and a personal relationship with Jesus to the community. They interceded and ask God to bless the Bible-believing churches and pastors.

In the midst of these prayers the Shekinah Glory fell. Suddenly, all the women were dancing a Prophetic Dance. Victory had come! God was revealing to each heart that their prayers had been heard and answered. That very week numerous testimonies were shared at Bible-believing churches. People who had been religious but had no personal relationship with Jesus had come to a saving knowledge of Christ. Every Bible-believing church in the area experienced growth in numbers.

The dancers were in tune with what God was doing. They had already heard from heaven. They knew what God had revealed to them through Prophetic Dance! God had heard their prayers and let them know the answer was on the way.

You may not be praying for revival in your area, but as you intercede for whatever the need may be, God may use you in Prophetic Dance. It's God's way of letting you know, "I've heard your prayers! I've seen your tears! The answer is on the way! Don't worry about that situation anymore! You've committed your way to Me and I've taken care of it! That burden is too heavy for you to carry, but not for Me! Let me be your burden-bearer. My shoulders are much broader than yours! Roll all your cares upon Me because I care for you."

Yes, Prophetic Dance is a dance of faith. We may not see it with our physical eye yet, but God has shown us through the "lens of faith" that it is done!

Chapter 4
Dance Lessons

Those who feel called to a ministry of dance should expect opposition. A dance ministry is so dynamic that it attracts spiritual attacks. Dancers must be full of the Word of God and sensitive to the leading of the Holy Spirit. Every dancer is enrolled in His school. The Holy Spirit has some dance lessons that He wants to teach each student. Live at the feet of Jesus in prayer and adoration. Staying close to Him will assure more power in your life and ministry of dance. There is no substitute for a life in the Spirit. No amount of practicing routines or purchasing expensive costumes can bring the anointing. Only time in His presence through prayer and Bible study will bring the results you long for.

Don't Look at Your Feet

As Christians, our focus and emphasis is always drawing all the attention toward our Heavenly Father and never toward the dancer. The eyes of the dancer are never on their feet, but always on the King. Remember God is after the dancer's heart, not the dancer's feet! The movements of Liturgical Dance are intentionally directed upward. Always conscious of the One being worshipped. Each dancer is physically up front performing, but inwardly hiding beneath the shadow of the Cross while ministering to the congregation. The emphasis is not glittery costumes, great talent or beauty. Although there is nothing wrong with honing one's dancing skills and becoming for Jesus the very best one can be, the main goal of the dancer is to give God all the glory, honor and praise. The dancers are yielded vessels of the Holy Spirit. Liturgical Dance brings an awesome awareness of God's presence. Heaven's floodgates are open and through this spiritual dance heaven visits earth.

In Liturgical Dance it is as if the dancer knows spiritual sign language. The dancers' movement brings the text to life. As the anointing rests on the dancers, a change takes place. God's holy presence fills the room. God is in the house! Dancers may use flags, banners, tambourines and other worshipping tools.

Order My Steps

Order my steps in thy word: and let not any iniquity have dominion over me. (Psalm 119:133 KJV)

The most important requirement to be a praise dancer is that you are in right standing with your Heavenly Father. Be sure that your personal walk with Jesus is genuine so that the eyes that watch you will see authentic worship. Your heart toward the Lord will determine the level of anointing that you will operate under. We must always remember that it's the anointing that breaks the yoke, and the Spirit of the Lord that sets us free!

How Beautiful Are the Feet of Them

As a minister of dance, you have something the world is searching for. God will see to it that hurting souls will be where you will be ministering. You are proclaiming "GOOD NEWS" to those bound and tormented. You know the One who can set them completely free! God may send you to minister hope and strength to a discouraged leader. God has anointed your feet! Your feet have been consecrated and sanctified for the Master.

How beautiful are the feet of those who bring good news! (Romans 10:15 KJV)

A discouraged pastor's wife, burned out from many busy years of ministry, attended a church service. She had not told one soul of her anemic spiritual condition, but the Holy Spirit knew. The service began. Many people were being blessed, but it seemed the Lord was passing her by. She was so numb from burnout that she couldn't even cry out to the Lord. Suddenly, the dancers showed up and began to lead in a beautiful Praise and Worship Dance. The Holy Spirit fell. Jehovah's Presence permeated the sanctuary. It was very apparent that they were all standing on holy ground. Something took place on the inside of that pastor's wife that will last throughout all eternity. When asked what exactly happened she replied, "It had something to do with the dancers being yielded to the Holy Spirit. As they obeyed the Lord through dancing, something broke on the inside of me. It was as if, while they were dancing, God was pouring 'strength for the journey' on the inside of me. I left that meeting able to meet the challenges that lay ahead of me. I knew it had something to do with the anointing and obedience of the dancers. I've never forgotten this life-changing experience and the crippling depression has never returned!"

We should not be surprised by the attacks of the enemy on the brothers and sisters fighting in ministry on the front lines. Our pastors and Christian leaders need the ministry of dance. In the Old Testament before David went to war, he sent the dancers and the singers out first to praise the Lord. Our pastors and Christian leaders are in the battle of their lives and need sanctified dancers to go before them and help them win the war.

Think Happy Feet

Here are a few tips to help keep your feet happy!

✓ Always wear comfortable shoes with a good arch support.

✓ Exercise on a regular basis. This will keep you in shape and help you not faint from sheer exhaustion when you minister in dance.

✓ Stay away from white flour and high calorie foods. Eat more fruits and vegetables. Work diligently to eat healthy foods so that you will maintain a healthy and comfortable weight easing the extra stress on your feet.

✓ Be sure that you stay hydrated. Drink plenty of pure water. Stay away from sugary drinks. Bring a water bottle to dance practice with you.

Dancing with Wolves

Take time to cover the entire dance team with prayer. During your prayer time allow the Holy Spirit to empty you of self and fill you to overflowing with His anointing. Prayer will help unite the dance group and diffuse any divisive attacks from the enemy. Realize that some of God's sheep have horns, and they just love to fight. Someone must be like Jesus in this situation. You be the one to be like Jesus! It may feel as if you are dancing with wolves some days, but if you keep loving and esteeming others higher than yourself, God will turn the wolves into lambs. Remember there is some wolf in each of us that the Lord is trying to cleanse out of us. God may be using another dancer to bring more victory in your own life and ministry. Stay united in Christ at all cost!

Make every effort to live at peace with all men. (Hebrews 12:14 NIV)

Ministry or Performance

Ministering in dance is not a performance. It is ministry! It's not something you do because you want to be seen or wear beautiful flowing garments. Lives are being impacted for all eternity by your dance ministry. Broken lives are being restored! Captives are being set free! There is unction and power as you yield your body to the Holy Spirit and dance under the anointing. It is a ministry! Not everyone will be appointed as a dancer, but the ministry of dance can minister to everyone. There will be those in the congregation who may never dance up in front, but they can be ministered to each time the anointed dancers begin to worship Him in dance. No one has to be left out from being touched by the Spirit of God.

Clear the Dance Floor

Be sure to check out the smallest details before you dance. The congregation needs to be able to get a clear view of each dancer. Dancing is a visual ministry. If possible, clear the dance floor. Attempt to remove any hindrances or distractions. Always ask permission first of the pastor or someone in charge before moving furniture or stage equipment.

Check out the lighting and see if you need to add additional lighting. Are you performing during a morning service or evening service? Is there enough natural light? Are there windows? Will the sun be shining through those windows at performance time? Do you need to add more light? Simple questions like these will help you be totally prepared and give the audience a positive experience.

Have a buddy system in place. Each "buddy" is responsible to check and recheck her dance partner to see if her garments fit right and if her makeup is applied correctly. It is easier to see another person's flaws. Remember when you are a buddy to be gracious and tactful if pointing out a problem area.

The director and an assistant should watch the performance during dress rehearsal. Four eyes are better than two at finding ways of improving and fixing any problems that might arise. Be sure to choose and assistant who has a constructive critical eye.

Chapter 5
Dance Instructor or Dance Student

You may feel called to be a dance instructor for the King or you may sense a calling to be a student of spiritual dance. Whatever the calling there are certain spiritual guidelines that, if followed, will help bring about a greater anointing and blessing of the Lord upon your life and ministry.

Your first call is not to ministry, but to JESUS! Keep falling in love with Him over and over again. This great love will cause a tremendous overflow of His Presence in your life and ministry. This anointing will spill onto the precious lives He chooses to bring you in contact with. You can't give others something you don't have, but if you have JESUS, you can give them JESUS!

Minister to God Before Ministering for God

Before any ministry rehearsals, spend time with Him. Seek His face! Allow your Heavenly Father to be your Dance Instructor! There are dances directly from His heart He desires to teach you. When His anointing falls, you will be dancing Spirit to spirit. His healing Spirit will touch the wounded spirit of those in the congregation. You may not know what anyone in the congregation has gone through before they came to the service, but the Holy Spirit knows. If you have spent time with Him, His "fingerprints" will be all over the worship from the beginning to the end. There is no substitute for time spent in prayer and His Word. The power does not come from great ability. The power comes from sitting at the feet of Jesus! This truth cannot be stressed enough. It is of utmost importance that a dancer minister to God before ministering for God!

Genuine Worship

Become transparent in your worship. Be genuine and authentic. You cannot fake the anointing! The anointing does not come from the ministry. The anointing comes because you have been with Jesus. God is looking for those who will worship Him in spirit and in truth.

God is a Spirit (a spiritual Being); and those who worship Him must worship Him in spirit and truth (reality). (John 4:24 AMP)

Prerequisites for Dance Ministry Members

There is a higher standard for those called into ministry. They are called to be set apart for the Lord. In the Old Testament we see how the Levites, who were ministers, had specific instructions from Jehovah.

...no one is to carry the ark of God but the Levites; for the Lord chose them to carry the ark of God, and to minister to Him forever. (1 Chronicles 15:2)

Levitical Call

Anointed dance worshippers have a Levitical call. *Levi* means joined. This represents the worshippers being joined to Christ with a consecrated loyalty and allegiance.

Levites Love God's House

Levites loved the House of the Lord. They lived closer to the Tabernacle than any of the other tribes. True worshippers will come into a "lovership" with Jesus. They will live closer to Him than the average Christian.

Number the sons of Levi by their fathers' households, by their families; every male from a month old and upward you shall number. The families of the Gershonites were to camp behind the tabernacle westward. The families of the sons of Kohath were to camp on the southward side of the tabernacle. And the leader of the fathers' households of the families of Merari was Zuriel the son of Abihail. They were to camp on the north side of the tabernacle. (Numbers 3:15, 23, 20, 35)

Anointed dance worshippers should exemplify excellence in their faithfulness to the House of the Lord. They should be punctual and a constant fixture in God's House. They should never neglect the House of the Lord. They make attending God's House a top priority for the rest of their lives!

Now these are those whom David appointed over the service of song in the house of the Lord, after the ark rested there. And they ministered with song before the tabernacle of the tent of meeting, until Solomon had built the house of the Lord in Jerusalem; and they served in their office according to their order. (1 Chronicles 6:31-32)

Discover the dance God has placed within you, and just as you never neglect the House of the Lord, you should never neglect the gift God has given you.

That is why I would remind you to stir up—rekindle the embers, fan the flame and keep burning—the (gracious) gift of God, (the inner fire) that is in you. (2 Timothy 1:6 AMP)

Levites are Useful and Fruitful

The (uncompromisingly) righteous shall flourish like the palm tree (be long-lived, stately, upright, useful, and fruitful); the righteous shall grow like a cedar in Lebanon (majestic, stable, durable and incorruptible). Planted in the house of the Lord, they shall flourish in the courts of our God. (Growing in grace) they shall still bring forth fruit in old age; they shall be full of sap (of spiritual vitality) and rich in the verdure (of trust, love and contentment); (They are living memorials) to show that the Lord is upright and faithful to His promises; He is my rock, and there is no unrighteous-ness in Him. (Psalm 92:12-15 AMP)

God's Word promises that the righteous (the Levites) shall be useful and bring forth fruit in their old age. What an exciting life! There is no age discrimination with God. We can never be too old for Him to use. God's Word says it, we believe it, and that settles it!

Levites Display a Teachable Spirit

Levites were to be mentored by and to serve under the high priest. Dance worshippers should serve under the leadership of a church. They should display a teachable spirit and be clothed in humility.

And I have given the Levites as a gift to Aaron and to his sons from among the sons of Israel, to perform the service of the sons of Israel at the tent of meeting, and to make atonement on behalf of the sons of Israel, that there may be no plague among the sons of Israel by their coming near to the sanctuary. (Numbers 8:19)

Levites Love to Serve

As ministers of the Good News, anointed dance worshippers are servants of the Most High. They are willing to do whatever God asks of them. They do not always have to be up front but are happy to work diligently behind the scenes. They love to serve their King in any capacity that He asks. Every dance worshipper must have a servant's heart.

Levites Surrender All

Dance worshippers are aware that they are consecrating their feet to the ministry God has called them to, but God asks for something more. He wants a consecrated lifestyle. Before Levites could begin their public ministry, they had to go through a cleansing ceremony.

Take the Levites from among the sons of Israel and cleanse them. And thus you shall do to them for their cleansing: sprinkle purifying water on them, and let them use a razor over their whole body, and wash their clothes, and they shall be clean. (Numbers 8:6, 7)

The Levites had to be sprinkled for cleansing. Each dance worshipper should be born again and experience the cleansing that can only come through the Blood of Christ.

Knowing that you were not redeemed with perishable things like silver or gold from your futile way of life inherited from your forefathers, but with precious blood, as of a lamb unblemished and spotless, the blood of Christ. (I Peter 1:18-19)

Each Levite had to shave his own flesh. Each dance worshipper should crucify all carnal fleshly desires so they will not be a stumbling block to the souls they minister to.

42

I have been crucified with Christ; and it is no longer I who live, but Christ lives in me; and the life which I now live in the flesh I live by the faith of the Son of God who loved me, and delivered Himself up for me. (Galatians 2:20)

The Levites had to wash their garments, ridding them of stubborn stains. Dance worshippers must strive to keep their minds renewed, not allowing the enemy to enter through the "mind gate." There may be times that another dance member does something that offends and hurts your feelings, causing your heart to become stained. Unforgiveness can be the most stubborn stain of all to try to remove from your soul. We must wash our garments with the Word of God and loving thoughts about our brother- or sister-in-Christ. Do not feed on unloving thoughts. Turn from them. Cover your mind with the precious powerful Blood of Christ. He will come to your rescue. *Forgive much, love much and criticize less* should be your heart's motto!

In reference to your former manner of life you lay aside the old self, which is being corrupted in accordance with the lusts of deceit, and that you be renewed in the spirit of your mind, that you put on the new self, which in the likeness of God has been created in righteousness and holiness of truth. Therefore, laying aside falsehood, speak truth, each one of you, with his neighbor, for we are members of one another. (Ephesians 4:22-25)

We read in the Old Testament that David only used the Levites who took the initiative to go through the sanctification process.

You are the heads of the fathers' households of the Levites; consecrate yourselves both you and your relatives, that you may bring up the ark of the Lord God of Israel, to the place that I have prepared for it. Because you did not

43

carry it at first, the Lord our God made an outburst on us, for we did not seek Him according to the ordinance. So the priests and the Levites consecrated themselves to bring up the ark of the Lord God of Israel. And the sons of the Levites carried the ark of God on their shoulders, with the poles thereon as Moses had commanded according to the word of the Lord. Then David spoke to the chiefs of the Levites to appoint their relatives the singers, with instruments of music, harps, lyres, loud-sounding cymbals, to raise sounds of joy. (I Chronicles 15:12-16)

Our Heavenly Father receives the honor due His Name more by a sanctified life than by great talent, costly dancewear or perfect choreography. Take time to be holy. Remember who you are representing. You are an ambassador for the King of Kings! Never do anything that would bring shame to His cause. There is no substitute for integrity. Be a dancer noted for your impeccable character. Let your personal testimony bring glory and honor to the Lord.

Chapter 6
Dance Studio

There are plenty of jobs in the Master's dance studio. While not everyone will be called to a dance ministry, this anointed ministry can minister to everyone. Just because you aren't up front ministering doesn't mean you cannot minister behind the scenes and help promote a dance ministry to your congregation. Consider heading up a Bible study to enlighten your church on the importance of spiritual dance in the Word of God. Invite a dance team to come and hold workshops teaching how spiritual dance could benefit your congregation.

Some of the key players who help make a dance ministry as productive as it can be are the pastor, the elders, the song worship leader, the dance instructor and the congregation.

The Pastor and The Elders

What a tremendous blessing when the pastor's and the elders' hearts are cemented with the love of God with the dance team. The gates of hell cannot prevail against a church that is united in heart and purpose. Ask the pastor and elders to pray for each member of the dance team. You need the leadership's covering. The leadership needs your ministry. United you stand! Divided you fall!

The Song Worship Leader

Song and dance ministries should fit together like a hand and glove. They should never be in competition with each other, but keenly aware that they are one body glorifying the one true God. The song worship leader should be familiar with basic dance terminology and theology. The dance instructor should work closely with the song worship leader. They should develop excellent communication skills so that there are no mix-ups during the worship service. The song worship leader should know when the dance will take place during the service, what signals will be given, what message the dancers are attempting to convey to the congregation and when the dance will end. The song worship leader should be prepared to take the congregation to a higher level of worship in response to the dance ministry.

The Dance Instructor

Dance instructors must have great leadership skills. They must also be clothed with the humility of Christ when dealing with the Dance Team or those in leadership. They have a very important role in being the resource person for the pastor and song worship leader in reference to what is happening with the dance ministry. They should communicate effectively so that the pastor, song worship leader and the congregation are aware of the dance programs offered in the church.

The dance instructor not only trains the dancers in dance, but also builds bridges between the dance team and leadership. The dance instructor leads by example and joyfully submits to spiritual authority. God is looking for "little" leaders. God will exalt those leaders who are little in their own eyes.

When you were small in your own sight, were you not made the head of the tribes of Israel, and the Lord anointed you king over Israel? (1 Samuel 15:17 AMP)

He must increase, but I must decrease—He must grow more prominent, I must grow less so. (John 3:30 AMP)

The Congregation

The leadership must be willing to educate the congregation about what God is doing through the dance ministry in the church. Remember, without the congregation there would be no dance ministry. Someone has to be sitting in the pews, inviting the broken-hearted and supporting the dance ministry in fervent prayer.

Encourage each member of the congregation to attend workshops, seminars or classes that teach on the importance of a dance ministry. The congregation should be taught to be attentive when the dancers are ministering, asking God to make them sensitive to the moving and wooing of the Holy Spirit, which will enable them to understand what God is doing in the service. The congregation should be the cheerleaders for their brothers- and sisters-in-the-Lord, as they minister in dance. When the worship leader invites the congregation to join in a congregational dance, the congregation should obey unless they have some health problems that would prevent them from doing so. They can show their support by standing, clapping or lifting their hands. Strive not to quench the Spirit.

A Time to Dance and a Time to Refrain from Dancing

The congregation must be taught that there will be certain times that they are not to dance along with the dance team. The worship leader would usually seat the congregation during this portion of the service. It would be inappropriate for members of the congregation to dance at this time. It would be as offensive as if they tried to sing while a soloist was singing or preach while the pastor was preaching. They must always be aware of any instructions given by the worship leader. Ask the Lord to speak to your heart as the dancers minister. Be ultra sensitive to what the Spirit of the Lord is doing in the service. The dance experience should lift you to a higher level of worship. When in doubt of what to do, follow the lead of the worship leader. This is an excellent time to learn to come under the leading of the worship leader. Many times someone feels that he or she knows more about the leading of the Lord than the worship leader. This is a form of pride and causes much division. Lead by example and follow the lead of the worship leader for the sake of unity.

By My Spirit Says the Lord of Hosts

To restore the Shekinah Glory through the ministry of dance to the church today is no small feat. We may have had great success in everything else we have put our minds to—organizing dance workshops, writing books on spiritual dance, getting big crowds out to come and see the dance team and preparing new dance routines. We must always remember the true source of success. It's not by talent, or by numbers, but His Spirit.

Not by might nor by power, but by My Spirit, says the Lord of hosts. (Zechariah 4:6)

In "His" Steps

There are certain dance steps that every praise dancer should be learning in the Master's dance studio. This comes through hearing the drumbeat of the Lord and stepping out into whatever He is asking. As we grow in this dance step we will see miracles happen before our eyes.

Stepping out in Love

Stepping out in God's love will keep you from stumbling. Failing to walk in love and feeding on unloving faults will cripple us. Let's be sure we are stepping out in love.

Great peace have they who love Your law; nothing shall offend them or make them stumble. (Psalm 119:165 AMP)

He has showed you, O man, what is good; and what does the Lord require of you, but to do justly, and to love kindness and mercy, and to humble yourself and walk humbly with your God. (Micah 6:8 AMP)

Keep out of debt and owe no man anything, except to love one another; for he who loves his neighbor—who practices loving others—has fulfilled the Law (relating to one's fellowmen), meeting all its requirements. (Romans 13:8 AMP)

Stepping out in Joy

Stepping out in the joy of the Lord will give you supernatural strength. Satan will use discouragement to try to entrap you or cause you to you stumble. Be wise to the enemy's tactics and stay full of the joy of the Lord. Keep a song in your heart and a dance in your feet at all times. Practice the Lord's Presence during the day. The Bible teaches us that there is fullness of joy in His Presence. Remind yourself in the midst of the storm that this too shall pass. Make every effort to be full of the joy of the Lord at all times.

The joy of the Lord is my strength! (Habakkuk 3:19 KJV)

You will show me the path of life; in Your presence is fullness of joy, at Your right hand there are pleasures for evermore. (Psalm 16:11 AMP)

...Weeping may endure for a night, but joy comes in the morning. (Psalm 30:5 AMP)

Stepping out in Peacemaking

For some this will be the most difficult dance step to learn, but this is a basic foundational block needed for your dance ministry. The enemy is sure to be defeated by practicing peacemaking techniques. Peacemaking will bring more power to your life and ministry.

Blessed are the peacemakers for they shall be called the sons of God. (Matthew 5:9)

Stepping out in Faithfulness

God rewards faithfulness. Remind yourself of this often. Be faithful to this ministry God has called you to. Victories will be won one dance at a time. Be faithful so you won't miss out on the victories God has just for you.

The Lord's lovingkindnesses indeed never cease, for His compassions never fail. They are new every morning; great is Thy faithfulness. (Lamentations 3:22-23)

These dance steps may seem too simple, but they are the beginning of an anointed, successful dance ministry. Some dancers have failed to learn these basic steps and found themselves shipwrecked. Be wise. Remember, some of the simplest and smallest footsteps leave the largest footprints in the souls of others. It won't be how many fancy dance steps you take, but the anointing under which you dance, that will leave indelible footprints behind.

Dancing Fundamentals

These dancing fundamentals will make you a team player and bring unity to your dance ministry team. They are very important and will bring a spiritual quality to your dance team. People are watching your steps. Be sure your steps are honoring the Lord. Make your life count so that it's difficult for someone else to fill your shoes. Be the best at loving others. Be a top-notch peacemaker. When people think of your life, may they think of faithfulness. If every member of your dance team would practice these dance steps, there would be no stopping the blessings of the Lord upon your life and ministry. Let's never neglect these dancing fundamentals.

Chapter 7
May I Have This Dance?

Jesus is extending an invitation for souls to dance for Him. These consecrated souls know that they are marching to the beat of heaven's drum. They are foreigners here. They are citizens of a heavenly kingdom not made with human hands. They have eternal vision. No longer do they believe the lies of the enemy. They have seen firsthand what anointed worship can do. They have tasted of precious Blood-bought victories. They have seen God use worship to destroy the works of the devil.

As the Body of Christ grows in their worship, they discover that worship involves shouting, singing, praising, lifting up of hands, bowing, standing and dancing. These are deep expressions of worship that God has ordained. Oh, how we need to be free so we can worship in great liberty.

Many ask, "What exactly will incorporating Holy Ghost worship do for me personally or for my church?" Once again we look to the Word of God and find He has the answers there for us.

Anointed Worship Makes Evil Spirits Depart

So it came about whenever the evil spirit from God came to Saul, David would take out his harp and play it with his hand; and Saul would be refreshed and be well and the evil spirit would depart from him. (I Samuel 16:23)

A seasoned minister was called to the home of a young woman who was being tormented by evil spirits. Her family had taken her to many church services and prominent doctors, trying to get help for her, but no help could be found. Then someone told them about this simple man of God who pastored a Spirit-filled church in New York. He was nothing to look at from the world's point of view, but those who knew him realized he walked closely with God. People all over had testified to the fact that he somehow could help those who were classified as being "hopeless" cases. Such was the case of this young woman. For years her family had been told that nothing more could be done for her. That is until they heard about how so many had received help through the prayers of this man of God. The pastor arrived at the family's house early in the afternoon. Just as soon as he walked through the doors, the evil spirits began to torment the young woman. The family started to fret as the young lady rocked back and forth and began grinding her teeth violently. The pastor asked the family to leave the room. The moment they left the pastor took a chair and sat down in it. He shut his eyes and waited a few moments in complete silence before the Lord. The young woman continued her rocking and grinding her teeth. Suddenly the pastor, led by the Holy Spirit, began to sing the Name above every name. He sang it over and over again. "JESUS! JESUS! JESUS! JESUS!" He swayed with his arms lifted singing the precious Name of Jesus! This went on for quite awhile. Then, he stopped. He stood to his feet and invited the family back into the room. To their utter amazement they found their daughter completely delivered. No longer was she grinding her teeth and rocking back and forth. She told them, "Jesus has set me free from my tormentor." The family began attending the church of that New York pastor. They discovered firsthand that anointed worship makes evil spirits depart.

Anointed Worship Transforms Defeat into Victory

Therefore, behold, I will allure her, bring her into the wilderness, and speak kindly to her. Then I will give her her vineyards from there, and the valley of Achor as a door of hope and she will sing there as in the days of her youth, as in the day when she came up from the land of Egypt. And it will come about in that day, declares the Lord, that you will call Me Ishi and will no longer call Me Baali. For I will remove the names of the Baals from her mouth so that they will be mentioned by their names no more. (Hosea 2:14-17)

Four years ago a dear sister-in-the-Lord was diagnosed with a very deadly type of breast cancer. Her mother had died prematurely from cancer. In fact, the woman was exactly the same age as her mother when her mother was diagnosed with cancer, and her mother only lived a few months longer. This dear sister had been raised to be very religious but never had a personal relationship with Jesus until just a few years previous. When the diagnosis came, she was given the best medical care available to her. She went to the renowned Mayo Clinic in Rochester, Minnesota. The doctors there told her that her prognosis was very poor. She was instantly defeated. She couldn't eat. She was unable to sleep. One thing she could do, however, was pray. So during those nights when she was attacked with great fear she would march around her home and began to praise the Lord for His faithfulness. She would thank Him for His healing touch. There were times the Holy Spirit would prompt her to dance right in her living room in the middle of the night. She yielded her body to the Lord and would dance and praise the Lord out loud. She knew God had touched her. She went back to her doctors and they were amazed at how well their "poor prognosis" patient was doing. She has never had a recurrence. She attributes her healing to God teaching her about the power of worship. Something supernatural takes place when you come into the Presence of God. Just this year this dear sister is starting a "Can-Cer-Vive (can survive) Tea Party Ministry" for other women who have had or have a loved one battling cancer. Her testimony is living truth that anointed worship transforms defeat into victory.

Anointed Worship Lifts a Defeated Spirit

To grant (consolation and joy) to those who mourn in Zion, to give them an ornament—a garland or diadem—of beauty instead of ashes, the oil of joy for mourning the garment (expressive) of praise instead of a heavy, burdened and failing spirit; that they may be called oaks of righteousness (lofty, strong and magnificent, distinguished for uprightness, justice and right standing with God), the planting of the Lord, that He may be glorified. (Isaiah 61:3 AMP)

The most amazing miracle that anointed worship does is bring the lifting power of the Holy Spirit to a downcast soul. It supernaturally lifts that soul up into heavenly places with Christ Jesus. One young man had been given to a spirit of living in the dumps. Moods just came over him and ruled his countenance, attitude and words. His dark moods made his marriage miserable and his children fear him. One day he saw in the Word of God that in "His" Presence is fullness of joy. Something settled in his heart. He began to pour over the Scriptures to see if there was help for his dark depression. He saw that the Word of God teaches us how to come into His Presence with thanksgiving and into His courts with praise. Light from Heaven permeated his soul. He wrote out a spiritual prescription plan for his darker side. He would get up every morning and praise the Lord out loud for fifteen minutes. He was not to kneel but to march and dance back and forth. The first couple days it was a breeze. He enjoyed praising the Lord out loud, but the third day the shadows had started to cover his soul. Darkness began to creep in. He remembered his promise he had made to His heavenly Father. He began to march back and forth and say out loud, "I will praise the Lord! I enter Your gates with thanksgiving and enter Your courts with praise." Suddenly he felt as if the Spirit of God were instructing him to lift up his hands toward heaven. He said that his arms felt like two large heavy hams. They did not want to be lifted up, but he obeyed what he felt the Spirit of God had asked him to do. The first ten minutes he felt foolish. Satan would whisper in his ear, "This isn't doing you any good. This is nonsense." But that young man obeyed and kept fighting the good fight of faith. Suddenly God's Presence filled the room. He began to laugh in the Spirit. The joy of the Lord filled him completely. That young man is now a middle-aged man and no one would ever describe him as moody. He is full of the joy of the Lord, and it's all because he discovered anointed worship lifts a defeated spirit.

Anointed Worship Brings His Glorious Presence

And when the trumpeters and singers were in unison, making one sound to be heard in praising and thanking the Lord, and when they lifted up their voice with the trumpets and cymbals and other instruments for song, and praised the Lord, saying, For He is good, for His mercy and lovingkindness endure forever, then the house of the Lord was filled with a cloud, so that the priests could not stand to minister because of the cloud; for the glory of the Lord filled the House of God. (2 Chronicles 5:13-14 AMP)

There is power in one person getting light and victory about anointed worship in his or her own personal life, but when you bring a whole church full of anointed worshippers, watch out! Miracles will take place. Demons will have to flee. Marriages will be restored. Broken hearts will be mended.

Roy Gray was the Dean of East Texas Bible College many years ago. He worked with many powerful Pentecostal evangelists. As he was teaching the students in his classroom, he often would share stories of his life's experiences. One story that he shared was about the famous evangelist Aimee Semple McPherson. Sister Aimee had large crusades. People from all walks of life would come to hear "Sister" preach. One night Angelus Temple was packed with people. As Sister stood to preach, God gave her a vision. She saw demons all across the sanctuary. They each carried a little pouch with some type of powder. They would sprinkle the powder over the members of the congregation. Then the people would begin to yawn and could hardly keep their eyes open. A holy indignation came over Sister Aimee. She began to lift her hands and praise the Lord out loud. She kept repeating, "Hallelujah! Hallelujah!" Every time she shouted, the demons would jump back. She called out to the congregation and told them what God had shown her and said that there were still demons in the sanctuary and asked them to all begin to lift their hands and worship the Lord together. Everyone stood and began to worship the Lord. Sister Aimee saw the evil spirits leave that place. Then there was a move of God in the meeting that never could have taken place with the enemy there. Oh, if God's people realized the weapon of anointed worship, they would promptly obey the Spirit of God.

Anointed Worship Releases the Word of the Lord

After that you will come to the hill of God, where the garrison of the Philistines is; and when you come to the city you will meet a company of prophets coming down from the high place with harp, tambourine, flute and lyre, before them prophesying. Then the Spirit of the Lord will come upon you mightily and you will show yourself a prophet with them; and you will be turned into another man. When they came to the hill (Gibeah), behold a band of prophets met him; and the Spirit of God came mightily upon him, and he spoke under divine inspiration among them. (I Samuel 10:5-6, 10 AMP)

Unfruitfulness in the church is often the result of quenching the Holy Spirit. Many people refuse to change and are not open to a deeper form of worship. We must lovingly and patiently share with those who misunderstand sacred dance that unfruitfulness will come if the Church despises what God loves. Go to the Word of God for all your answers. This will help those who might not quite understand sacred dance to settle some questions they have. A good story to share with them is the story of David dancing before the Lord with all his heart, and how his wife Michal despised him in her heart. This despising resulted in Michal being barren from that day until her death.

So David went and brought up the ark of God from the house of Obededom into the city of David with rejoicing. And when those who bore the ark of the Lord had gone six paces, he sacrificed an ox and a fatling. And David danced before the Lord with all his might, clad in a linen ephod (a priests upper garment). So David and all the house of Israel brought up the ark of the Lord with shouting, and the sound of the trumpet. As the ark of the Lord came into the city of David, Michal, Saul's daughter, (David's wife), looked out of the window, and saw Kind David leaping and dancing before the Lord and she despised him in her heart. They brought in the ark of the Lord, and set it in its place inside the tent, which David had pitched for it; and David offered burnt offerings and peace offerings before the Lord. When David had finished offering the burnt offerings and peace offerings he blessed the people in the name (and presence) of the Lord of hosts, and distributed among all the people, the whole multitude of Israel, both to men and women, to each a cake of bread, a portion of meat, and a cake of raisins. So all the people departed, each to his house. Then David returned to bless his household. And (his wife) Michael, daughter of Saul, came out to meet David, and said, How glorious was the king of Israel today, who stripped himself of his kingly robes and uncovered himself in the eyes of his servants' maids, as one of the worthless fellows shamelessly uncovers himself! David said to Michal, It was before the Lord, who chose me above your father and all his house, to appoint me as prince over Israel, the people of the Lord. Therefore will I make merry (in pure enjoyment) before the Lord. I will be still more lightly esteemed than this, and will humble and lower myself in my own sight (and yours); but by the maids you mentioned I will be held in honor. And Michal, the daughter of Saul had no child to the day of her death." (2 Samuel 6:12-23 AMP)

Chapter 8
Garments of Praise

The Bible instructs us as to what spiritual garments are to be worn.

...And all of you, clothe yourselves with humility toward one another for God is opposed to the proud, but gives grace to the humble." (1 Peter5:5)

The Word of God also teaches what sacred garments are to be worn by the Levites in the midst of the congregation.

And you shall make for Aaron your brother sacred garments (appointed official dress set apart for special holy services) for honor and for beauty. You shall make for them (white) linen trunks to cover their naked flesh, reaching from the waist to the thighs. And they shall be on Aaron and his sons when they go into the tent of meeting, or when they come near to the altar to minister in the holy place, lest they bring iniquity upon themselves and die; it shall be a statute forever to Aaron and to his descendants after him." (Exodus 28:2, 42-43 AMP)

A spiritual dancer dresses to honor God. A dancer's whole emphasis is to glorify Him. Our dress/attire should never be a stumbling block to the observer or worshipper.

Dancers also dress for beauty. The costumes enhance the worship experience. The sacred garments are appointed dress for a special holy service.

Many dance ministries have consecrated their "garments of praise" to the Lord. The garment is special because it should only be tastefully worn for the purpose intended. The garment must be handled with great care. It should not be treated like any other article of clothing. Your garments of praise should be dedicated to the Lord and always used for that purpose. You should not just wear your garments of praise anywhere. They should be worn only for ministry.

One handmaiden of the Lord had ministered in dance at a church. She was a fairly new Christian, but felt her entire wardrobe had changed since coming to Christ. She had danced for the world wearing leotards and tights, but when she became a believer and began dancing for the Lord, she added conservative blouses and skirts to her leotards and tights. She felt she was very modest but had been praying if there was anything in her ministry that would cause one to stumble that God would reveal it to her. After a dynamic worship service in which she had danced, she heard that two men on the back pew snickered every time she whirled, causing her skirt to come up. She immediately went to the Lord and cried, "Lord, I've already put a skirt and blouse on, what else can I do?" At that very moment the Lord birthed an idea in her heart. She designed a pair of sacred dance culottes that had just the right amount of flair to keep them from hanging down like bloomers and yet remedied the problem. She then felt free to minister to the glory of God.

What to Wear

Undergarments: Do wear a good support bra and shape wear. Investing in these items will set one free to move in a manner that is almost unexplainable. Male dancers should wear an athletic jockey support. Be sure that all your undergarments fit properly and are a solid color. Make slips and camisoles part of your regular costume. It is better to err on the side of modesty than to cause a brother or sister to stumble.

Dresses, Skirts, Blouses: Don't wear any garment that is low cut or tight. No midriff tops or blouses should ever be worn. Dresses with slits should not be worn. No see-through clothes should be allowed on the dance floor. Remember, you may stretch or bend; be sure your dress or skirt is not too short. If you spin, it is best not to wear full skirts.

Slacks: Be sure that slacks fit properly and are not too tight.

Mirror Inspection

Do a check-up in the mirror to see if your clothes pass inspection. Move around, bend over and wave your arms. This simple exercise can spare you some embarrassment. Avoid anything that would be sexually suggestive whether in dress or dance movements.

Sacred Garments

A few of the key factors to consider when investing in dancewear for your dance ministry are modesty, convenience and price. You want to have quality merchandise at a reasonable expense. The garments of praise you choose will reveal to the congregation the love, beauty and character of God. There are many dance distributors available because of the tremendous growth of dance ministries. Proper attire will help you to relax with confidence and focus more on your ministry.

Colors of Dance

Being knowledgeable about the significance of the colors you wear and the colors you use with your banners, ribbons, hoops or tambourines can enhance your dancing ministry.

- **Gold** represents Kingship, Majesty, the Godhead, the glory of Heaven, righteousness, trial by fire, mercy

- **Silver** represents God's gifts, wisdom, purity, redemption, the Word of God

- **Bronze** represents truth, justice, judgment, fires of testing

- **Blue** represents heaven, the priesthood, grace, water, cleansing, the Holy Spirit

- **Green** represents creation, new life, growth, prosperity, restoration, God's holy seed, harvest, swing and reaping

- **Red** represents salvation, the Blood of Jesus, cleansing justification, sin, consuming fire, the cross

- **Purple** represents kingdom authority, dominion, royalty, kingship, power and grace

- **White** represents holiness, purity, cleansing, the Bride of Christ, surrender, angels, saints, triumph, victory and glory

- **Black** represents darkness, evil, sin, death, famine, affliction, humiliation and sadness

- **Yellow** represents joy, celebration, light, glory revealed and faith

- **Pink** represents healing, health, right relationships, compassion, heart of flesh and passion for Jesus

- **Orange** represents passion, power, fire, harvest season, fruitfulness, joy and the Holy Spirit

- **Turquoise** represents sanctification, River of God and the New Jerusalem

- **Amber** represents the Father's heavenly care, fiery passion, flaming throne of God, God's glory, wisdom and the temple of God

A combination of colors can bring about a visual effect that will bring more power to the message you are trying to get across. An example of this would be to combine gold and blue symbolizing the Royal Deity. Red and white can represent the cleansing Blood of our Savior upon a soul. Combining red, orange and yellow gives the appearance of a blazing fire, symbolizing the fire of the Holy Spirit, who wants to burn out any impurities in our lives.

If we take time to dig into the Word of God, we soon discover that God uses colors as symbols. Let's take a look at some of the colors in the Holy Scriptures.

Colors in the Bible

Red and White: Come now, and let us reason together, says the Lord; though your sins be as scarlet, they shall be as white as snow; though they be red like crimson, they shall be as wool. (Isaiah 1:18 Amplified)

Green: They will still yield fruit in their old age; they shall be full of sap and very green. (Psalm 92:14)

Silver: My son, if you will receive my sayings, and treasure my commandments within you, make your ear attentive to wisdom, incline your heart to understanding; for if you cry for discernment, lift your voice for understanding; if you seek her as silver and search for her as for hidden treasures; then you will discern the fear of the Lord, and discover the knowledge of God. (Proverbs 2:1-5)

Blue, Gold, Purple and White: And Mordecai went forth from the presence of the king in royal apparel of blue and white, with a great crown of gold, and with a robe of fine linen and purple, and the city of Shushan shouted and rejoiced. (Esther 8:15 AMP)

Black: "And I say, and behold, a black horse, and in his hand the rider had a pair of scales (a balance)." (Revelation 6:5 AMP)

White: "Let us rejoice—and shout for joy—exulting and triumphant! Let us celebrate and ascribe to Him glory and honor, for the marriage of the Lamb (at last) has come and His bride has prepared herself. She has been permitted to dress in fine (radiant) linen—dazzling and white, for the fine linen is (signifies, represents) the righteousness—the upright, just and godly living (deeds, conduct) and right standing with God—of the saints (God's holy people)." (Revelation 19:7-8 AMP)

We see in these Scriptures that God uses color to get his point across. Let us, as praise worshippers use colors to get His point across, also.

Chapter 9
Called to Dance

Dance ministries are exploding all over the world. The call has gone forth from heaven that God's people should dance. Invisible chains are being broken as the anointed dancers are becoming more like Jesus and dancing under the power of the Holy Ghost. Young children are being "raised to praise" their Creator through dance. Men and women are obeying the call to praise Him in dance.

There will always be those who sit on the fence and debate whether or not their church should attempt to develop a dance ministry at their church. Change is sometimes difficult for those who get stuck in a rut of doing things the same, year after year. Here are a few tips on how to get a dance ministry started in your church for those who feel called to dance!

Find a Dance Instructor

The first priority is to find someone to lead the dance worshippers. This does not have to be someone who has majored in dance. It could be someone who used to lead an aerobics class and has a good sense of movement, rhythm and a heart for people. It could be someone who was a cheerleader in high school and has a gift of movement and rhythm.

The dance instructor should also have a scrvant's heart and have the heart of a worshipper. The emphasis should always be Jesus, but the instructor should consistently be working on dancing skills and artistry.

Ease into a dance ministry by starting slow and simple. Don't attempt to dance to something that is way over your dance team's level of ability. You want to strive for a polished look, not a pitiful one. Start with a powerful song and work on signing some of the words and simple dance steps. Be creative, but simple!

Lighting is very important, but don't worry if your church doesn't have professional lighting. Once again, be creative. Try turning down the houselights and strategically placing other lights for the desired affect. Practice makes perfect. Practice! Practice! Practice! Repetition will always be your best teacher.

There are many Christian schools of dance or workshops that the dance instructor and the dance team can attend. Some of the workshop ministries will come to your home church and help answer any questions you may have concerning starting a dance ministry. Some charge minimal fees. Do your homework. Look around and find the ministry that meets the needs of your congregation.

Dance Curriculum

Worship Dance is the medium of the hour in the church today. When taught properly, each dancer will learn how to make the anointed music become visual to the congregation.

A dance instructor should be ministering to the body, soul and mind of the worship team. With the teachings in this book, the dance instructor should be able to minister with confidence the Word of the Lord. Following are some tips for dance instructors:

Body

Develop movement and technique through basic dance steps. Learn basic movements and use them over and over again. Then add new movements to expand your knowledge of various dance steps.

Practice foot and arm patterns over and over until every dancer feels confident! Don't be in a hurry to learn new moves. Remember, repetition is the best teacher. Go at the speed of your slowest dancer. The extra practice will make everyone more confident. If your dancers don't feel confident and make a lot of mistakes, they may never get up front again because of the humiliation, but if you have your dance team ready and prepared, they will minister to the very best of their ability for many years to come.

Practice group patterns until the group dances as one body! This is so important. The dance team needs to have one heartbeat. They need to move as one body. This takes lots of practice. Some singers feel that they have perfected a song after they have performed it at least one hundred times. They seem to grow in confidence because they know where the high notes are. They know when they need to take a breath. They have the words memorized. They know their part. They have become so familiar with the song that sometimes they find the melody constantly playing in their head. Every dancer needs to become so familiar with their dance steps that they are dancing in their sleep. It has been said that the way to tell if a person has mastered a new language is to ask them what language they dream in. If they dream in the language they are learning, it is a sign that they have finally mastered the language. The same principles apply to perfecting dance steps. You become so sure of the movements that there are no awkward movements. All the dancer's movements are fluid. This can only come about by much repetition and practice. The old saying is still true today. Practice makes perfect!

Mind

Memorizing scripture. The dance instructor should have a scripture for each dance practice for the entire dance team to memorize. Then when the dance team comes together, the team should recite the scripture out loud together. Choose scriptures that reflect what God is teaching the dance team. If some of the members are struggling with confidence, choose scriptures that encourage and strengthen them. If you are in deep spiritual warfare, choose scriptures that will boost the morale of the dance team. Scriptures that will build their faith and cause them to feel that there is victory in the camp. By building up the inner spirit of each dancer, the dance instructor is giving the dance team a sense of unity. And the gates of Hell cannot prevail against God's people when there is unity.

Creating simple yet flowing choreography will enhance your dance team's ministry. Something that is beautiful to watch causes the dancers to feel beautiful as they dance for their King.

It's so important that every dancer be teachable, even if the dance instructor is younger than the dancers. God has placed the dance instructor over the dancers. It's so important that they have a covering. And it's very important that each dancer learns to yield to authority. This will help them in yielding to the Lord when He asks them to do something they might not want to do. We must all learn to lay down our wills for Jesus just as He did for us!

Spirit

The dance team that prays together stays together. The dance instructor must have appointed prayer times with the dance team. Each dancer has an invisible enemy who wants to see you fail, but each dancer has an invisible Friend who wants to see you prevail. If we knew the power of prayer, we would be more faithful to pray. Be sure that your dance ministry is birthed and bathed in prayer.

The dance instructor must feed the spirit of the dancers. There must be Bread in the House of the Lord for the hungry. The dancers should never minister spiritually empty. Emptiness can cause bizarre behavior. It is up to the dance instructor to be feeding them the Word of God. The dance instructor should be giving a solid foundation and biblical teaching on developing a worship dancer's heart.

The dance instructor must teach each dancer that they are not living in two worlds. Dancers shouldn't be talking like they want to talk outside of the dance ministry and then come to "perform" for the church and have a whole different set of words. No! Each dancer must be taught that they are to develop worship as a lifestyle. Carefulness in the home! Carefulness in the meeting! We want to be the same person on the platform as we are off the platform. If you walk in the Spirit outside of the meeting, you will dance in the Spirit inside the meeting. There will be a higher level of anointing as you develop a deep sensitivity to what the Holy Spirit is trying to speak to you. This comes by living in the Spirit outside the meeting. God may speak to you through a dream the night before you are to minister in dance. Many times He may let you know what He wants to do in a service before you ever get there, but this only comes to those who have developed a spiritual antenna with the Holy Spirit. Many others may be clueless, but do not have to be. As you cultivate a sincere heart of worship, lives will be changed for all eternity.

Facial Expressions

Always keep in mind that facial expressions are extremely important. An element that can improve facial expression is always being conscious of where your eyes are at any given time. This dance technique is called focus. Usually the eyes should follow the hand movements. What power there is when a dance team's focus is all the same! There is something about the unity of heart, soul and body that generates a higher level of anointing. If hands are extended upward representing the Lord, eyes should gaze upward, too. Always keep the focus where the focus needs to be. A visual harmony will occur that will move the congregation and bring glory to the Lord. The congregation can feel if the worship is coming from the dancer's heart. The hand movements and footwork may be superb, but there is no substitute for a true heart of worship. What is taking place on the inside of the worshipper will show up on the outward facial expressions.

Spiritual Sensitivity

There is a holy boldness that each child of God should walk in. We should not fear when we are being led in a new way. This applies to sacred dance, too.

Do not call to mind the former things, or ponder things of the past. Behold, I will do something new, now it will spring forth; will you not be aware of it? (Isaiah 43:18-19)

We need this holy boldness to go forth in the power of the Holy Spirit, but what if we are just beginning in a dance ministry? Maybe we belong to a church that hasn't really embraced a dance ministry. Fear not! There are steps that the dance team can take to help ease the congregation into embracing and supporting the new ministry God has given them. God can help you win the hearts of the congregation by applying a few key principles.

Winning the Dance Contest

Dance to a familiar moving song. Something that strums the heartstrings!

If the church is more traditional, think traditional in songs and movements!

Be loving and patient, and don't argue about dance.

Let the invisible power of God's love win the battle for you.

Keep your life clean so that you won't give the opposition any ammunition to use against your dance ministry.

Song Selection

One of the most important elements of a dance ministry is choosing the right song. This cannot be stressed enough. Here are a few points to consider when choosing a song for your dance team to minister to.

Understand the Words. Be sure that every word can be understood! Clarity of words is a must for ministry purposes. You are a visual sermon with visual harmony. Don't choose a song where the congregation cannot understand the message.

Biblical Message. Be sure that the song is in total agreement with the Word of God. We live in a day and age when just because it says it's a "Christian" song doesn't necessary mean it is. The Bible says that His Word will not return empty. If you are dancing to a song with biblical foundations, your dance is not in vain. We can never go wrong with keeping our feet planted on the Rock.

"So shall My word be which goes forth from My mouth; it shall not return to Me empty, without accomplishing what I desire, and without succeeding in the matter for which I sent it. For you will go out with joy, and be led forth with peace; the mountains and the hills will break forth into shouts of joy before you, and all the trees of the field will clap their hands. Instead of the thorn bush the cypress will come up; and instead of the nettle the myrtle will come up; and it will be a memorial to the Lord, for an everlasting sign which will not be cut off." (Isaiah 55:11-13)

Anointed Message. Choose songs that move you. A song that has an anointed message and that draws people in to the Presence of God the minute they hear it. Remember miracles take place when "He" shows up. The emphasis is always Jesus Himself!

Pleasant Melody. If you are just introducing a dance ministry to your congregation, try to choose songs with a pleasant melody. A song that appeals to a vast audience will help make your biggest critics your biggest fans.

Flowing Movements. Be sure that your song selection allows you to transpose words into flowing movements. There are some songs that are powerful, but when you attempt to put them to choreography, they just don't work. Be sensitive to this and choose songs that are danceable.

Song Selection Questions. Each member of the dance ministry should bring a pen and spiral notebook to the dance practices. The dance instructor should ask the following questions, allowing time for each dancer to write down their answers. At the end of the questioning, there should be discussion about how each member answered the following questions. This will keep you from wasting your valuable time and choosing the wrong songs and also help the dance team to be in unity as they see and hear how the song ministered to each one. Play the song for the dance team and then answer these questions. The dance instructor should answer the questions, too.

Dance Questionnaire

1. Write down one word that this song made you think about! (Powerful? Victorious? Prayerful?)

2. How did the song make you feel?

3. What type of dance song is it? (Prophetic? Intercessory? Lyrical? Liturgical? Celebration?)

4. Does the song have a strong biblical message? If so, what is that message?

5. Who would this song minister to?

6. What type of crowd would this song appeal to?

7. How danceable is this song?

8. Did this song minister to you personally?

9. Do you feel this song is a good fit for our dance ministry?

10. If our dance team approves this song, will you commit to pray every day for God to use this song for His glory as we minister in dance?

Choreography Tips

For heartfelt movements, you must step out of your own shoes and into the shoes of the songwriter. This is what makes your dance ministry a ministry and not just a performance. Take time to close your eyes and feed upon each lyric line. How does it affect your life personally? How does it make you feel? Get a good grip on what the songwriter is trying to get across. Once you have a sense of what the message is, then you can add facial and body expressions that will enhance the song. Concentrate on lyric lines rather than every word. Allow your movements to crescendo as the song builds and fall as the song falls.

There are no shortcuts to a spiritually, physically and emotionally healthy dance ministry. Biblical principles must be adhered to. Following these simple instructions will help your dance ministry to prosper and flourish and minister to all who the Lord brings across your path.

Beloved, I pray that you may prosper in every way and (that your body) may keep well, even as (I know) your soul keeps well and prospers." (3 John 1:2 AMP)

Chapter 10
Reign Dance

The King's daughter is all glorious within; her clothing is interwoven with gold. She will be led to the King in embroidered work; the virgins, her companions who follow her, will be brought to Thee. They will be led forth with gladness and rejoicing; they will enter into the King's palace. In place of your fathers will be your sons; you shall make them princes in all the earth. I will cause Thy name to be remembered in all generations; therefore the peoples will give Thee thanks forever and ever. (Psalm 45:13-17)

Not many of us believe we have ever met a princess, yet they are all around us. You are the King's daughter. God is thrilled to make every daughter of His a royal princess. Look at the other women on your dance team and tell them often, "You are the King's daughter!" Build them up with your words of affirmation.

As you begin your dance ministry, you will discover very quickly that you are walking where angels fear to tread. You will experience satanic attacks, but you don't have to fear. Our King of Kings promises in His Word when the enemy comes in like a flood He will raise up a standard against him. The battle belongs to the Lord.

So (as a result of the Messiah's intervention) they shall (reverently) fear the name of the Lord from the west, and His glory from the rising sun. When the enemy shall come in like a flood, the Spirit of the Lord will lift up a standard against him and put him to flight—for He will come like a rushing stream which the breath of the Lord drives. (Isaiah 59:19 AMP)

Do not fear or be dismayed because of this great multitude, for the battle is not yours but God's. (2 Chronicles 20:15)

There are generational curses and strongholds that won't die easily. Remind yourself as you experience attacks from the enemy that you are the King's daughter and no weapon formed against you shall prosper.

No weapon that is formed against you shall prosper. (Isaiah 54:17)

There are certain enemies that might rear their ugly heads and hiss at you; you will have to turn to Jesus and begin to worship Him through a "Reign Dance." Satan will tell you that you cannot start or be in a dance ministry. At this point you must remember that You are the King's daughter and He is making you more than a conqueror.

Yet amid all these things we are more than conquerors and gain a surpassing victory through Him Who loved us. (Romans 8:37 AMP)

Let's look at some of the enemies the King of Kings will help you defeat and reign over in complete victory.

The King Reigns Over Discouragement

The enemy of discouragement has defeated many souls. He is a sly enemy and comes in when we least expect him. We must put on the whole armor of God and be wise and discerning. When we feel the shadows of "I can't start a dance ministry! I'm too old! God can't use me. I'm just a nobody! Our church is too small!" we must stop what we are doing and begin quoting who we are in Christ.

I can do all things through Him who strengthens me. (Philippians 4:13)

The story is told of the demons in Hell having a meeting. Their target was a godly woman who was beginning a ministry of dance in her conservative church. Satan was trying to figure out how he could stop her. He promised a promotion to the demon that could come up with a successful plan to stop her from her mission.

One cross-eyed imp grunted, "I know what to do, Master! I'll get her to go back to the ways of the world. I'll tempt her with booze and drugs."

Satan growled at his darkened servant, "You idiot! She won't go back to her old ways. She's fallen too in love with her Lord."

Another cohort choked, "I know what to do, Master! I'll tempt her with her old boyfriends and get her to fall into immorality."

Satan barked, "You imbecile! She won't be tempted by those old ways. She's too thankful to be forgiven and free from the pain of the past!"

A pigeon-toed, hunched-back demon slithered his way to Satan's feet. "I know what to do, Master! I'll discourage her soul!"

Satan jumped with glee and squealed, "Brilliant plan! I think it will work!"

We must be wise to the enemy's tactics. Discouragement is one of his weapons. Stay in the Word of

God and don't let discouragement reign over you, but allow Christ to reign over discouragement in your life.

The King Reigns Over Strongholds

And Abraham said of Sarah his wife, She is my sister. (Genesis 20:2 AMP)

So Isaac stayed in Gerar. And the men of the place asked him about his wife, and he said, She is my sister; for he was afraid to say, She is my wife, thinking, lest the men of the place should kill me for Rebekah; because she was attractive and was beautiful to look upon. (Genesis 26:6-7 AMP)

The familiar story of Abraham lying to save his own skin has a lesson for each one of us. Then years later we find Isaac committing the very same sin. Our King desires to reign over generational curses and strongholds that the enemy wants to use to destroy us, but if we live in God's Word and put on the whole armor of God, the enemy will be defeated and those generational curses will be snapped in two.

In conclusion, be strong in the Lord—be empowered through your union with Him; draw your strength from Him—that strength which His (boundless) might provides. Put on God's whole armor of a heavy-armed soldier, which God supplies—that you may be able successfully to stand up against (all) the strategies and the deceits of the devil. For we are not wrestling with flesh and blood—contending only with physical opponents—but against the despotisms, against the powers, against (the master spirits who are) the world rulers of this present darkness, against the spirit forces of wickedness in the heavenly (super-natural) sphere. Therefore put on God's complete armor, that you may be able to resist and stand your ground on the evil day (of danger), and having done

*all (the crisis demands), to stand (firmly in your place).
Stand therefore – hold your ground – having tightened the
belt of truth around your loins, and having put on the
breastplate of integrity and of moral rectitude and right
standing with God; and having shod your feet in
preparation (to face the enemy with the firm-footed
stability, the promptness and the readiness produced by the
good news of the Gospel of peace. Lift up over all the
(covering) the shield of saving faith, upon which you can
quench all the flaming missiles of the wicked (one). And
take the helmet of salvation and the sword of the Spirit
wields, which is the word of God." (Ephesians 6:10-17
AMP)*

*Be of sober spirit, be on the alert. Your adversary,
the devil prowls about like a roaring lion, seeking someone
to devour. (1 Peter 5:8)*

The King of Kings is the only One who can bring
complete victory over generational curses. He desires to
reign in your own personal life and ministry.

The King Reigns Over Pride

Another enemy that wants to defeat you is a spirit of
pride. This foe takes on many forms. He can show up when
you least expect him. He relies on the dancer's ability,
talent, skill or expertise, and doesn't feel a need for Christ's
anointing. Pride will show up when someone, possibly in
leadership, criticizes you by whispering in your ear, "What
do they know? Who do they think they are? I can take 'my'
dance ministry to the church down the road. I don't need
their covering."

One minister of dance tells a story of how blessed
she was when she first started dancing for the Lord. Many
people came up and expressed how wonderfully she had
done. She started believing that she was better than any

other dancer she had seen. Of course, she never said that out loud where anyone could hear, but in her heart she felt she had more anointing and more skill.

One day she ministered in a large church and was greeted with intense applause. As she left the platform, an elderly woman met her at the back of the church.

The elderly woman hugged the dancer and said, "I would tell you that you are the most anointed and most beautiful dance minister I have ever seen, but I sense Satan has already told you that."

Something broke in the dancer's spirit. She wept before the Lord and repented of her sin of pride. God went on to use her in phenomenal ways, and she never again leaned on her own ability.

God resists the proud but gives grace to the humble. (I Peter 5:5 KJV)

One seasoned saint had been to see a dance ministry in a large city. He left the meeting and exclaimed, "Oh, what mighty dancers!" Then the following Sunday he attended another church where a dance team ministered. He left that meeting crying, "Oh, what a Savior!"

Oh, my dear friend, may the dance ministry you are a part of be for the glory of God!

I am the Lord; that is My name, and My glory I will not give to another. (Isaiah 42:8 AMP)

May the King of Kings reign over every vestige of pride that lurks in our souls.

As you win victories for the Kingdom of God, you will find you will be dancing on holy ground. Lives are changed when they have been with the King. Wherever the King makes an appearance is holy ground! As you allow the King to reign in your soul, He will defeat your enemies and every dance will be a "Reign Dance!"

Chapter 11
Dance Props

We will (shout in) triumph at your salvation and victory, and in the name of our God we will set up our banners; the Lord fulfill all your petitions." (Psalm 20:5 AMP)

We serve a creative God. He loves variety. God can use banners, flags, tambourines and other dance props to give your dance ministry more power. These props are not meant to replace your current methods of worship, nor are they any better. They are just another creative way God has ordained to express your love for Jehovah. It's a prophetic fulfillment.

Again I will build you, and you shall be rebuilt, o virgin of Israel! Again you shall take up your tambourines, and go forth to the dances of the merrymakers. Again you shall plant vineyards on the hills of Samaria; the planters shall plant and shall enjoy them. For there shall be a day when watchmen on the hills of Ephraim shall call out, Arise, and let us go up to Zion, to the Lord our God. (Jeremiah 31:4-6)

As has been our custom throughout this book, let's look into the Word of God and settle it in our hearts that banners and tambourines may be used in worship.

Flags and Banners in the Bible

Taking our Strong's concordance, we find these Hebrew words used in the Old Testament for flags or banners. (The reference numbers are in parenthesis.)

DEGEL (1713/1714) to be conspicuous, to raise a flag, setting up with banners

NACE (5251) a signal, a flag, a token – banner, a standard

OWTH (226) a signal, as a flag, a beacon, mark, sign

Let's take a look into the Word of God and discover *how banners are used.*

Banners Declare Allegiance

Banners reveal the group or place you identify with, whether it is your family, country or even an Olympic team. They show to whom you declare your allegiance. They connect people for a common cause or action.

The Israelites shall encamp each by his own (tribal) standard, or banner, with the ensign of their fathers' houses, opposite the tent of meeting and facing it on every side. (Numbers 2:2 AMP)

In that day the heir to David's throne will be a banner of salvation to all the world. The nations will rally to him, for the land where he lives will be a glorious place. He will raise a flag among the nations for Israel to rally around." (Isaiah 11:10, 12 NLT)

Banners Bestow Honor

Banners are used to bestow honor to important dignitaries who may come for a visit.

Go out! Prepare the highway for my people to return! Smooth out the road; pull out the boulders; raise a flag for all the nations to see. The Lord has sent this message to every land: "Tell the people of Israel, 'Look, you Savior is coming. See he brings his reward with him as he comes.'" (Isaiah 62:10-11 NLT)

Banners Communicate

Banners herald an important event. A banner is a visible object. When a president passes away, our country bestows honor by flying the American flags at half-mast. It communicates to all who see it that someone very important to our nation has died, and we honor him by showing our grief.

In a dance ministry, banners can communicate God's message to the Church.

When I raise my battle flag on the mountain, let all the world take notice. (Isaiah 18:3 NLT)

Banners can be a Point of Contact for Healing

So the Lord sent poisonous snakes among them, and many of them were bitten and died. Then the people came to Moses and cried out, "We have sinned by speaking against the Lord and against you. Pray that the Lord will take away the snakes." So Moses prayed for the people. Then the Lord told him, "Make a replica of a poisonous snake and attach it to the top of a pole . . . Whenever those who were bitten looked at the bronze snake, they recovered. (Numbers 21:6-9 NLT)

The Lord may send desperate souls into the very place where you're ministering in dance. They may need spiritual, emotional or physical healing. As you lift up the banner, it is a visual for healing to take place just as Moses lifted up the serpent and all who looked upon it were healed. Banners can be a point of contact for miracles to take place. We may never fully understand God's methods, but we can trust His heart and leading in our lives. If He is leading you to use banners in your dance ministry, learn all you can about them. Learn the significance of the colors and emblems. Teach what you have learned to the rest of the team. This will create a holy confidence as you minister before the congregation. Don't be ashamed. Declare the glory of the Lord!

Banners Unify the Troops

Banners call the armies together. A banner flying encourages soldiers to fight to the death. The banner becomes the point of focus and the troops rally when they see the flag they are fighting for waving bravely.

See the flags waving as the enemy attacks. Cheer them on, O Israel! Wave to them as they march against Babylon to destroy the palaces of the high and mighty. (Isaiah 13:2 NLT)

Banners Send the Enemy Packing

Even their generals will quake with terror and flee when they see the battle flags. Says the Lord, whose flame burns brightly in Jerusalem. (Isaiah 31:9 NLT)

The dance ministry God is calling you into is about spiritual warfare. There is an enemy of our souls, but we need not fear. God has given us mighty weapons to defeat our foe. Using banners in a dance ministry will send the devil packing as you minister in the Holy Ghost.

Banners Claim Victories Won

This is what the Lord says: "Tell the whole world, and keep nothing back! Raise a signal flag so everyone will know that Babylon will fall!" (Jeremiah 50:2 NLT)

But you have raised a banner for those who honor you—a rallying point in the face of attack. (Psalm 60:4 NLT)

Banners are set up like trophies in His Name. He has already won the battle for us. Dance in victory for the King!

Symbolism in Banners

As you begin to use dance props in your ministry, be sure to take the time to understand the symbolism concerning the fabrics, trims and jewels. This will bring you into a deeper level of worship.

Apple: Sin, temptation

Bells: High Priest wore bells as he ministered in the temple. Also symbolic of praise and worship

Brocade: Fabric worn by kings

Budded Cross: Trinity

Butterfly: Resurrection, new life, beginning again

Candle: Jesus—the Light of the World

Circle Entwined with Triangle: Trinity

Cross: Jesus' victory over death

Crown: Crown of glory, crown of life, crown of righteousness, Jesus, King over all the earth, Heaven's Prince, victory

Diamonds: Enduring, of great value, the saints of God

Dove: Holy Spirit

Dove with Olive Branch: Peace

Eagle: Flying to place of protection, intimacy with God

Flame: Holy Spirit, burning out the dross, cleansing power

Flowers: Fruitfulness of God's children, Jesus—Rose of Sharon, Lily of the Valley

Glittering Stones: God's light, the glory of God

Heart: Devotion

Heart with cross: God's love

Keys: Spiritual authority over spirit realm

Lamb: Jesus—the sacrificial Lamb

Lamp: Wisdom and knowledge

Lily: Resurrection, triumph over death

One Candle: Unity

Palm Branches: Victory, adoration, triumph over death

Pearls: Pearl of Great Price

Rainbow: God's promises, covenant

Serpent: Temptation, sin, the fall of man

Soldier's Armor: Spiritual Warfare, Armor of God

Star of David: God's people

Sun: Jesus—Son of Righteousness

Sword: Armor of God

Tassels: Holiness, reminder to obey God's commandments

Three Candles: Trinity

Trumpet: Call to worship

Symbolism in Banner Motions

- ✓ A figure '8' made three times is the equivalent of the Name of Jesus. (The Greek spelling of Jesus is IESOUS, I=10, E=8, S=200, O=70, U=400, S=200; 10+8+200+70+400+200=888.)

- ✓ Wrapping the banner around the pole and unwinding it can represent releasing the anointing.

- ✓ Waving the banner from side to side can represent God's glory.

- ✓ Waving the banner in a circular motion above your head can represent saying, "Lord, send down Your glory!"

✓ Holding a banner high above your head and marching is considered a way of announcing, "There is victory in the camp!"

✓ Intense, forceful movements with banners are symbolic of spiritual warfare.

✓ Flowing, swaying movements with banners are symbolic of adoration and worship.

Hebrew word for Tambourine

Another dance prop with a biblical history is the tambourine. Many servants of the Lord have been used mightily under the power of the Holy Spirit as they danced and played their tambourine.

TOPH (8596) *tambourine, timbrel, tabret*

TAPHAPH (8608) *play on the tambourine, play with timbrels*

The tambourine was used in ancient times in warfare and to celebrate victories. In the Bible it speaks of the tambourine being used in praise and worship.

David and all the people of Israel were celebrating before the Lord with all their might, singing songs and playing all kinds of musical instruments—lyres, harps, tambourines, castanets and cymbals." (2 Samuel 6:5 NLT)

Singers are in front, musicians are behind; with them are young women playing tambourines. (Psalm 68:25 NLT)

Sing! Beat the tambourine. Play the sweet lyre and the harp. (Psalm 81:2 NLT)

Dancing with the Tambourine

Praise his name with dancing, accompanied by the tambourine and harp. (Psalm 149:3 NLT)

Praise him with the tambourine and dancing. (Psalm 150:4 NLT)

I will rebuild you, my virgin Israel. You will again be happy and dance merrily with tambourines. (Jeremiah 31:4 NLT)

God's Methods

God's methods are different from man's. Our minds must be renewed by the power of the Holy Spirit. We are too carnally minded! We must grow in the Lord and learn the Laws of His Kingdom. In His Kingdom if you want to be great, you must learn to be a servant. The way up is to kneel low at His feet in humility.

Instead, God deliberately chose things the world considers foolish in order to shame those who think they are wise. And he chose those who are powerless to shame those who are powerful. God chose things despised by the world, things counted as nothing at all and used them to bring to nothing what the world considers important, so that no one can boast in the presence of God. (1 Corinthians 1:27 NLT)

We must remind ourselves of the story of David and Goliath. Goliath laughed when he saw the puny boy come to meet him with a slingshot and five smooth stones. But God chose to use a little shepherd boy and one small stone to defeat Goliath. You, too, are a giant-killer! God has called you into a ministry that may look foolish to the world, but it is not foolish to God.

Symbolic Weapons

We all realize that the stone did not have some magical power, but it was the instrument God chose to use to slay the giant. There are no magical powers in the dance props God may have you use to defeat the enemy, but they hold deep symbolism. When you begin to worship and praise the Lord in singing and dance with a heart that is right before Him, the enemy is being defeated. You are a warrior in the Army of the Lord.

Blessed be the Lord, my rock and my keen and firm strength, Who teaches my hands to war and my fingers to fight. (Psalm 144:1 AMP)

You are entering a war zone! There will be times of testing ahead, but there will be more times of precious victories that help you to grow and develop into the person of God He wants you to be.

Take (with me) your share of the hardships and suffering (which you are called to endure) as a good (first class) soldier of Jesus Christ. (2 Timothy 2:3 AMP)

Onward Christian soldiers!

Pastor Roberts Proclaims the Word of God

From Another Level – DANCING!!!

Dancing Ushers My Soul Into a Place of Freedom

Dancing with the Banner is New and Exciting!!!

My Soul Looks Up To Thee

Lord, I Lift Your Name On High

I Find Happiness and Joy in God's Presence

Dancing For God After Fifty Is a Joyful Experience

Pastor Roberts is a *Soaring Eagle*

Pastor Roberts Loves Her Husband of 30 Years, Elisha

They Celebrated Their 50th Birthday Together

Chapter 12
Victory Dance

Soldiers know that there is always a great price for freedom. They realize that men and women have laid down their lives for their country so that people could be free. Freedom costs something! Freedom means someone laid down his or her life so someone else could taste and experience victory.

You are a soldier for the King. As you go forward in your dance ministry, you will soon discover that there are days you will be laying down your life for your brothers and sisters-in-the-Lord. As you travail in prayer, praise and spiritual dancing, Jesus will be setting people free. Let's look and see how God may bring a "victory dance" into these lives.

Victory Comes Through Praise

One of the most powerful weapons of warfare you will ever discover is the power of praise. Praise brings the anointing and the anointing breaks the yoke!

...And the yoke shall be destroyed because of the anointing. (Isaiah 10:27 KJV)

People ask how they can have God's anointing in their lives. The answer is very simple. Fall in love with Jesus! Spend time with Him. Get to know Him. Live in the Word of God. Practice His Presence. Sing to Him! Shout to Him! For you to have an anointed dance ministry and victorious Christian life you need to know something about the power there is in praise. A story that has helped many throughout the years is the story of Jehoshaphat.

And Jehoshaphat stood in the assembly of Judah and Jerusalem, in the house of the Lord, before the new court, and said, O Lord, God of our fathers, are You not God in Heaven? And do You not rule over all the kingdoms of the nations? In Your hand are power and might, so that none is able to withstand You. Did not You, O our God, drive out the inhabitants of this land before Your people Israel, and give it forever to the descendants of Abraham Your friend? They dwelt in it, and have built You a sanctuary in it for Your name saying, If evil comes upon us, the sword of judgment or pestilence, or famine, we will stand before this house and before You, for Your name (and the symbol of Your presence) is in this house, and cry to You in our affliction, and You will hear and save. And now behold the men of Ammon, Moab, and Mount Seir, whom You would not let Israel invade when they came from the land of Egypt, and whom they turned from and did not destroy. Behold, they reward us by coming to drive us out of Your possession, which You have given us to inherit. O our God, will You not exercise judgment upon them? For we have no might to stand against this great company that is coming against us. We do not know what to do, but our eyes are upon You. And all Judah stood before the Lord, with their children and their wives. Then the Spirit of the Lord came upon Jahaziel son of Zechariah, son of Benaiah, son of Jeiel, son of Mattaniah, a Levite of the sons of Asaph, in the midst of the assembly. He said, Hearken, all Judah, you inhabitants of Jerusalem and you King Jehoshaphat, the Lord says this to you: Be not afraid or dismayed at this great multitude; for the battle is not yours but God's. Tomorrow go down to them; behold they will come up by the ascent of Ziz; and you will find them at the end of the ravine before the wilderness of Jeruel. You shall not need to fight in this battle; take your position, stand still, and see the deliverance of the Lord (Who is) with you,

O Judah and Jerusalem. Fear not, nor be dismayed; tomorrow go out against them, for the Lord is with you. And Jehoshaphat bowed his head with his face to the ground, and all Judah and the inhabitants of Jerusalem fell down before the Lord, worshipping Him. And the Levites, of the Kohathites and Korahites, stood up to praise the Lord God of Israel with a very loud voice. And they rose early in the morning and went out into the wilderness of Tekoa; and as they went out, Jehoshaphat stood and said, Hear me, O Judah, and you inhabitants of Jerusalem, believe in the Lord your God, and you shall be established; believe and remain steadfast to His prophets, and you shall prosper. When he had consulted with the people, he appointed singers to sing to the Lord and praise Him in their holy (priestly) garments, as they went out before the army saying, "Give thanks to the Lord, for His mercy and lovingkindness endure forever!" And when they began to sing and praise, the Lord set ambushments against the men of Ammon, Moab and Mount Seir, who had come against Judah, and they were (self) slaughtered. (2 Chronicles 20:5-22 AMP)

The people cried, "We don't know what to do but our eyes are upon You." Dear friend, you, too, will have situations come up in your life and ministry that you do not know what to do. The greatest secret that you could ever discover is to keep your eyes on Jesus. If we keep our hearts right and our eyes upon Him, He will fight our battles for us.

For though we walk in the flesh, we do not war after the flesh; for the weapons of our warfare are not carnal, but mighty through God to the pulling down of strong holds; casting down imaginations, and every high thing that exalteth itself against the knowledge of God, and bringing into captivity every thought to the obedience of Christ; and having a readiness to avenge all disobedience when your obedience is fulfilled. (2 Corinthians 10:3-6 KJV)

Victory Comes Through a Sanctified Thought Life

Many times the enemy of our soul enters through the "mind" gate. Keep the mind gate closed to Him. One sure way to do this is each day cover your mind with Jesus' Blood. Another way is think on the things God has commanded us to.

Finally, brethren, whatever is true, whatever is honorable, whatever is pure, whatever is lovely, whatever is of good repute, if there is any excellence and if anything worthy of praise, let your mind dwell on these things. (Philippians 4:8)

And do not be conformed to this world, but be transformed by the renewing of your mind, that you may prove what the will of God is, that which is good and acceptable and perfect. (Romans 12:2)

...We are taking every thought captive to the obedience of Christ. (2 Corinthians 10:5)

Victory Comes Through Obedience

As we learn the truths in God's Word, we will see that victory always comes through obedience. The best kind of obedience is prompt obedience. Prompt obedience is the very best way to show that you believe. Let us obey promptly and as we do God will pour out more blessing and anointing in our own personal lives and ministry.

...And we are ready to punish all disobedience. (2 Corinthians 10:6)

...Behold, to obey is better than sacrifice, and to heed than the fat of rams. (1 Samuel 15:22)

As we sow these biblical principles into our life, we are promised a bountiful harvest.

Do not be deceived, God is not mocked; for whatever a man sows, this he will also reap. For the one who sows to his own flesh shall from the flesh reap corruption, but the one who sows to the Spirit shall from the Spirit reap eternal life. And let us not lose heart in doing good, for in due time we shall reap if we do not grow weary." (Galatians 6:7-9)

Chapter 13
Types of Dance Warriors

God needs warriors and not weaklings in his army. There are three different types of dance warriors. This has to do with the Levitical Call. It has to do with the way that you will function in God's army. Discovering your call will help you find your place and the giftedness God has given you.

Scouts

Scouts are the first type of dance warriors. They sometimes can be known as spies. They are designed to run reconnaissance.

Moses sent them to scout out the land of Canaan, and said to them, Get up this way by the Negeb (the South) and go up into the hill country, and see what the land is, and whether the people who dwell there are strong or weak, few or many, and whether the land they live in is good or bad, and whether the cities they dwell in are camps or strongholds, and what the land is, whether it is fat or lean, whether there is timber on it, or not. And be of good courage, and bring some of the fruit of the land. Now the time was the times of the first ripe grapes. (Numbers 13:17-20 AMP)

If you are called to be a scout you will have a keen sense of discernment. God will reveal things to you during the service. It may be that God shows you one person in the congregation who is weak and needing a touch from the Lord. If you are visiting a church, God may supernaturally show you some of the strongholds in that church. The scouts have a large Gift of Discernment.

Scouts gather information. Not to gossip or to be puffed up with too much knowledge, but they gather information to report back to the leaders so they can plan the next military step. Scouts on a dance team may report to their leaders some areas of concern that need to be covered with prayer and fasting. Scouts can be trusted to only give secret information to their leaders. They don't discuss their findings with others.

Scouts usually gather information by going into the enemy's camp. It can be dangerous work. The dance ministry God is calling you into is not for cowards. You will be doing battle with the devil. He does not give up easily. But we know that greater is He that is in you than he that is in the world.

There may be pockets of resistance in a meeting where you are ministering. Scouts will be able to zero in on the problem, but they need the other warriors to bring complete victory to the situation.

Warning to the Scouts

Sometimes a scout may become fainthearted and bring defeat to what the Lord is attempting to accomplish. Feed on the Word of God so that you will be built up and not have a weak spot for the enemy to bring you down.

Caleb quieted the people before Moses, and said, Let us go up at once and possess it; we are well able to conquer it. But his fellow scouts said, "We are not able to go up against the people (of Canaan); for they are stronger than we are. So they brought the Israelites an evil report of the land which they had scouted out, saying, The land, through which we went to spy it out, is a land that devours its inhabitants; and all the people we saw in it are men of great stature. (Numbers 13:30–33 AMP)

The scouts began to speak fear to the whole congregation of Israelites. They were to report to only the leaders privately. But because a spirit of fear gripped their hearts, this is what happened.

And all the congregation cried out with a loud voice, and (they) wept that night. All the Israelites grumbled and deplored their situation, accusing Moses and Aaron, to whom the whole congregation said, Would that we had died in Egypt! Or that we had died in the wilderness! Why does the Lord bring us to this land, to fall by the sword? Our wives and little ones will be a prey; is it not better for us to return to Egypt? And they said one to another, Let us choose a captain and return to Egypt. Then Moses and Aaron fell on their faces before all the assembly of Israelites. And Joshua son of Nun and Caleb son of Jephunneh, who were among the scouts who had searched the land, rent their clothes; and they said to all the company of Israelites, The land through which we passed as scouts is an exceedingly good land. If the Lord delights in us, then He will bring us into this land and give it to us, a land flowing with milk and honey. (Numbers 14:1-8 AMP)

Because of the scouts' report the Israelites had to wander in the wilderness for forty years. A scout should never go beyond their leaders. If they do, there can be devastating loss.

Take the call of being a scout very seriously. It is an important and strategic position in the Army of God.

Watchmen

The second type of calling is that of a watchman. A watchman declares what he sees. He can call out warnings or announce from his tower, "Twelve o'clock and all's well!"

The mournful, inspired prediction – a burden to be lifted up – concerning the desert of the sea (which was Babylon after great dams were raised to control the waters of the Euphrates River which overflowed it like a sea, and would do so again). As whirlwinds in the South (the Negeb) sweep through, so it (the judgment of God by hostile armies) comes from the desert, from a terrible land. A hard and grievous vision is declared to me; the treacherous dealer deals treacherously, and the destroyer destroys. Go up, O Elam (here put for Persia)! Besiege, O Media! All the sighing (caused by Babylon's ruthless oppressions) I will cause to cease (says the Lord). Therefore all my (Isaiah's) loins filled with anguish; pangs have seized me like the pangs of a woman in childbirth; I am bent and pained so that I cannot hear, I am dismayed so that I cannot see. My mind reels and wanders, horror terrifies me. (In my mind's eye I am at the feast of Belshazzar; I see the defilement of the golden vessels taken from God's temple; I watch the handwriting appear on the wall, I know that Babylon's great king is to be slain). The twilight I looked forward to with pleasure has turned into fear and trembling for me. They prepare the table, they spread the rugs, and having set the watchers (the revelers take no other precaution), they eat, they drink. Arise you princes, and oil your shields (for your deadly foe is at the gates)! For thus has the Lord said to me, Go, set (yourself as) a watchmen, let him declare what he sees. (Isaiah 21:1-6 AMP)

A watchman declares what he sees. There are times that he may see the enemy trying to wiggle his way into the camp. There might be times in your dance ministry that God is moving and you feel victorious. But you must remember this: When God starts blessing, the devil starts messing! Satan will plan strategic attacks upon your ministry. This is where the watchman can be a great blessing. The watchman can come to the leadership and let them know that something is wrong. We are not talking about a spirit of criticism. A watchman is very loyal. He is completely consecrated to the ministry God has placed him in. When he comes to sound his warning he comes in simplicity, humility, sincerely and in truth. It is possible for the problem to be coming from inside the church. A watchman is able to see it and sound the alarm before any damage is done.

Hark, your watchmen lift up their voice, together they sing for joy; for they shall see eye to eye the return of the Lord to Zion. (Isaiah 52:8 AMP)

Son of man, I have made you a watchman to the house of Israel; therefore hear the word at My mouth, and give them warning from Me. (Ezekiel 3:17 AMP)

I have set watchmen upon your walls, O Jerusalem, who will never hold their peace day or night; you who (are His servants and by your prayers) put the Lord in remembrance (of His promises), keep not silence, and give Him no rest until He establishes Jerusalem and makes it a praise in the earth." (Isaiah 62:6-7 AMP)

It is the job of the watchman to always be on guard. The watchman recognizes some of the tactics of the enemy. This warrior does not take it lightly if someone is spreading gossip, knowing that gossip could be just the weapon that causes the fatal blow to the ministry. The watchman squashes any backbiting. All members of the dance ministry are safe under the watchman's care. They watch each other's backs because of the watchman's warnings.

The watchman knows that division in the ministry will make it less effective.

Because of the stand the watchman takes against what carnal Christians call harmless habits, this warrior is usually not very popular. People pleasers don't make good watchmen. Watchmen must have the heart of the lamb but the hide of a rhinoceros. They must have hearts for the Body of Christ, and be able to take intense criticism.

Also I set watchmen over you, saying, Hear and obey the sound of the trumpet. (Jeremiah 6:17 AMP)

The Spirit of the Lord shows the watchmen when the enemy is coming. So, to get the dancers' attention the watchmen has to, at times, be more intense on his warning. He may have to "blow his trumpet" or point out to the team an area where the enemy is trying to get in. The watchman recognizes that he will one day stand before God and have to give an account if he did his job to the best of his ability.

Pray for the prophetic watchman in your dance ministry. This is not an easy calling. Ezekiel had to live among scorpions as he prophesied, trying to warn God's people. The watchmen won't have to live among scorpions, but some of the people of God the watchman is called to warn will have a poisonous stinger—their tongues. So cover this warrior in your prayers and heed the watchman's warnings.

And you, son of man, be not afraid of them, neither be afraid of their words; though briers and thorns are all around you and you dwell and sit among scorpions, be not afraid of their words, nor be dismayed at their looks, for they are a rebellious house. (Ezekiel 2:6 AMP)

The watchmen can be the loneliest of all the warriors. They need our prayer cover. The Lord shows them things before the common foot soldier sees that there is a problem. Love your watchmen. Support them and God will bless you for it.

Armor-Bearer

The last type of warrior that every dance ministry needs is an armor-bearer. This warrior is filled with the humility of Christ. His job is vital but not glorious. We all recognize that in a spiritual battle we need to put on the whole armor of God. If we don't, we won't be able to stand against the devil. The armor is a defense. It covers the warrior's vital internal organs. The breastplate covers the heart. The helmet covers the skull, and the shield if for quenching the fiery arrows. The armor-bearer is the person God has raised up in your defense. The armor-bearer of a dance team is the one who is covering you spiritually.

The devil will do his best to strip you of all your armor. It is the duty of every spiritual armor bearer to get a sword to you if you drop it, or if you lose a piece of armor, your armor-bearer is right there to remedy the problem and be sure that your are properly equipped.

The outstanding character traits of this warrior are love and loyalty.

And David came to Saul, and served him. Saul became very fond of him, and he became his armor-bearer. (I Samuel 16:21 AMP)

An armor-bearer is so filled with the love of God that this mighty warrior will go out in harm's way and help another warrior without any need for recognition or praise. When the war is over and the victory won, the other warrior might receiver the honor instead of the armor-bearer, but without the armor-bearer's aid the other warrior might have been utterly destroyed.

One day Jonathan son of Saul said to his armor-bearer, Come, let us go over to the Philistine garrison, on the other side. But he did not tell his father. Saul was remaining in the outskirts of Gibeah under a pomegranate tree in Migron; and with him were about 600 men, and Ahiah son of Ahitub, Ichabod's brother, son of Phinehas, son of Eli, the Lord's priest in Shiloh, wearing an ephod. And the people did not know Jonathan was gone. Between the passes by which Jonathan sought to go over the Philistine garrison, there was a rocky crag on the one side and rocky crag on the other side; one was named Bozez, and the other Seneh. The one crag rose on the north in front of Michmash, and the other on the south in front of Geba. And Jonathan said to his young armor-bearer, Come, and let us go over to the garrison of these uncircumcised; it may be that the Lord will work for us; for there is nothing to prevent the Lord from saving by many or by few. And his armor-bearer said to him, Do all that is in your mind; I am with you in whatever you think (best). Jonathan said, We will pass over to these men, and we will let them see us. If they say to us, Wait until we come to you, then we will stand still in our place, and will not go up to them. But if they say, Come up to us, we will go up; for the Lord has delivered them into our hand, and this will be our sign. So they both let the Philistine garrison see them. And the Philistines said, Behold, the Hebrews are coming out of the holes where they have hid themselves. The garrison men said to Jonathan and his armor-bearer, Come up to us, and we will show you a thing. Jonathan said to his armor-bearer, Come up after me, for the Lord has given them into Israel's hand. Then Jonathan climbed up on his hands and feet, his armor-bearer after him; and the enemy fell before Jonathan and his armor-bearer killed them after him. And that first slaughter, which Jonathan and his armor-bearer made, was about twenty men, within about a half acre of land, which a yoke of oxen might plow." (I Samuel 14:1-14 AMP)

Jonathan's armor-bearer was always thinking of Jonathan ahead of himself. Jonathan did not fight all by himself, but his loyal armor-bearer fought right beside him helping the one he loved. He was more aware of Jonathan's battle than his own.

These warriors in a dance ministry will be loyal to each member of the dance team. They will help pray for each dancer earnestly, longing for victory to come as if they were praying for themselves. With this warrior in your army, you can be sure major victories will be won.

And ten young men, Joab's armor-bearers, surrounded and struck Absalom, and killed him. (2 Samuel 18:15 AMP)

Don't think that every dance ministry can have only one armor-bearer, or one scout or one watchman. There can be more than one in a dance ministry. Every dancer should operate as an armor-bearer to someone. Many armor-bearers have a call to restore hurt or injured warriors back to health. Some warriors have been severely wounded. The armor-bearer would lovingly apply the Balm of Gilead on their wounds.

The armor-bearers will help the dance team always be prepared by seeing they are dressed in full battle gear. The gates of Hell cannot prevail against a dance ministry that is in full battle gear.

The weakness of an armor-bearer is that they might grow weary in the work of love. This is where the watchmen can possibly warn the armor-bearers that discouragement is approaching or that extra rest is needed. The scouts, also, can sometimes see something coming before the armor-bearers. This is because the armor-bearers are in the heat of the battle and working so closely with each warrior that they sometimes aren't aware of the enemy's tactics unless their fellow warriors have warned them.

There is coming a day when the warriors shall be able to rest. There will be a day when the fighting is over, but right now we are in a Holy War. We must have our loins girded with truth. We must fight for the souls of men. The churches you will be dancing in will have drug dealers, prostitutes, the brokenhearted, alcoholics and many other sin chains that have the souls of men and women bound for generations. You must be alert! Your lives must have the power of the Holy Spirit so that there is nothing between your soul and the Savior. And as you dance under the anointing of the Holy Spirit, you will see souls born into the kingdom of God. Chains will be broken. The enemy will be defeated. Lives will be transformed. We are at war with the enemy. Don't take your ministry lightly.

Forward! March!

Chapter 14
Fox Trot

Catch the foxes for us, the little foxes that are ruining the vineyards. (Song of Solomon 2:14)

Little foxes cannot play in a vineyard unless they do some damage to the fruit. They cause the vines to snap and the fruit falls to the ground, ruining the vineyards. Many people may feel that the little foxes are so cute and that they are not doing any harm, but we see that it's the little foxes that are ruining the vineyards. How can it be that something so small and trivial can wreak havoc? It's because little sins never stay little.

In your dance ministry you must not allow the little foxes to spoil what God is trying to do in your life and ministry. Some people may be able to get away with certain behaviors, but God is raising the bar and asking you to come up to higher ground. You are no longer your own. God has paid a great price to purchase you. Don't allow the little foxes to ruin the plan that God has for you! We must remove the little foxes that creep into our vineyards. Make those little foxes do the fox trot out of the vineyard of your life and ministry and not wreak havoc in the spiritual destiny God has for you!

A Soothing Aroma

Then Noah built an altar to the Lord, and took of every clean animal and of every clean bird and offered burnt offerings on the altar. And the Lord smelled the soothing aroma. (Genesis 8:20-21)

Therefore be imitators of God, as beloved children; and walk in love, just as Christ also loved you, and gave Himself up for us, an offering and a sacrifice to God as a fragrant aroma. But do not let immorality or any impurity or greed even be named among you, as is proper among saints; and there must be no filthiness and silly talk, or coarse jesting, which are not fitting, but rather giving of thanks. For this you know with certainty, that no immoral or impure person or covetous man, who is an idolater, has an inheritance in the kingdom of Christ and God. Let no one deceive you with empty words, for because of these things the wrath of God comes upon the sons of disobedience. Therefore do not be partakers with them; for you were formerly darkness, but now you are light in the Lord; walk as children of light. For the fruit of the light consists in all goodness and righteousness and truth), trying to learn what is pleasing to the Lord. And do not participate in the unfruitful deeds of darkness, but instead even expose them; for it is disgraceful even to speak of the things, which are done by them in secret. But all things become visible when they are exposed by the light, for everything that becomes visible is light. (Ephesians 5:1-13)

What fragrance does your life and ministry emit to God? There is no substitute for Godly living. The best thing to do if you have sin in your life is to repent and make your wrongs right. Put off the unfruitful deeds of darkness. They will ruin your ministry. Don't bring shame to the work of the Lord by allowing sin to reign in your life. Live a life that brings glory to the Lord. He gave His very best for you. Give your very best for Him.

Sin will always take you further than you want to go. Sin kills everything it touches. Sin will destroy the testimony of a ministry. You cannot be too careful. Don't allow the little foxes to come in and ruin the vineyard of the Lord. May your ministry never bring shame to our Master.

And Such Were Some of You

Don't let sin have dominion over you. You may have been a slave to sin in the past, but now you've been washed by Jesus' Blood. Flee from sin! Jesus has set you completely free so dance for Jesus in purity and holiness of life.

If the Son therefore shall make you free, ye shall be free indeed! (John 8:36 KJV)

Or do you not know that the unrighteous shall not inherit the kingdom of God? Do not be deceived; neither fornicators, nor idolaters, nor adulterers, nor effeminate, nor homosexuals, nor thieves, nor the covetous, nor drunkards, nor revilers, nor swindlers shall inherit the kingdom of God. And such were some of you; but you were washed, but you were sanctified, but you were justified in the name of the Lord Jesus Christ, and in the Spirit of our God. (1 Corinthians 6:9-11)

Aching Feet

You will discover as you begin your dance ministry that the worst enemy of enthusiasm is time. People have a way of getting tired of wonderful things. We all can think of things that once excited us, but now our joy has faded. Children get tired of their new toys, billionaires get tired of their money and Christians get tired of doing good. When you first began the dance ministry, you were excited and couldn't wait to learn a new song and minister wherever the Lord opened the door, but over time something changed. We must not grow weary in doing God's will.

And let us not be weary in well doing; for in due season we shall reap, if we faint not. (Galatians 6:9 KJV)

There will be days that you feel as if you are going through the motions. Stay faithful. God rewards faithfulness. Stand upon the promises of God. He promises that we shall reap if we faint not. No matter how much your feet ache with discouragement, keep dancing! Someone needs your dance. Remember God's faithfulness to you. You be faithful to God. God will give you strength. When you find you are losing heart, that's when you need to stop what you are doing and find the King. Spending time with the King will change your perspective. Only time in His Presence can dispel shadows and expel the weaknesses of the flesh. Come boldly to His throne where you will find grace to help in your time of need.

Let us then fearlessly and confidently and boldly draw near to the throne of grace – the throne of God's unmerited favor (to us sinners); that we may receive mercy (for our failures) and find grace to help in good time for every need – appropriate help and well-timed help, coming just when we need it. (Hebrews 4:16 AMP)

But they that wait upon the Lord shall renew their strength; they shall mount up with wings as eagles; they shall run and not be weary; and they shall walk, and not faint. (Isaiah 40:31 KJV)

A Servant's Heart

Now before the Passover Feast began, Jesus knew (was fully aware) that the time had come for Him to leave this world and return to the Father. And as He had loved those who were His own in the world, He loved them to the last and to the highest degree. So during supper, Satan having already put the thought of betraying Jesus in the heart of Judas Iscariot, Simon's son, Jesus knowing (fully aware) that the Father had put everything into His hands, and that He had come from God and was (now) returning to God, got up from supper, took off His garments and

117

taking a (servant's) towel, He fastened it around His waist. Then He poured water into the washbasin and began to wash the disciples' feet and to wipe them with the (servant's) towel with which He was girded. When He came to Simon Peter, (Peter) said to Him, Lord, are my feet to be washed by You?—Is it for You to wash my feet? Jesus said to him, You do not understand now what I am doing, but you will understand later on. Peter said to Him, You shall never wash my feet! Jesus answered him, Unless I wash you, you have no part with (in) Me – no share in companionship with Me. Simon Peter said to him, Lord, (wash) not only my feet, but my hands and my head, too! Jesus said to him, any one who is bathed needs not to wash except his feet, but is clean all over. And you (My disciples) are clean, but not all of you. For He knew who was going to betray Him; that was the reason He said, You are not all of you clean. So when He had finished washing their feet and had put on His garments and had sat down again, He said to them, Do you understand what I have done to you? You call Me the Teacher (Master) and the Lord, and you are right in doing so, for that is what I am. If I then, your Lord and Teacher (Master), have washed your feet, you ought—it is your duty, you are under obligation, you owe it—to wash one another's feet. For I have given you this as an example, so that you should do (in your turn) what I have done to you. I assure you, most solemnly I tell you, A servant is not greater than his master, and no one who is sent is superior to the one who sent him. If you know these things, blessed and happy and to be envied are you if you practice them—if you act accordingly and really do them." (John 13:1-17 AMP)

The sure way to have a blessed life and ministry is to follow our Lord's example and be a servant-leader who leads by example.

- ✓ Jesus rose from supper and later He rose from the dead! He asks you to rise and dance for Him. Rise and be a part of what He is doing in the earth. Rise to a new level in Christ. Don't continue to live for the base things of life. Rise to a higher calling! Let us follow our Master and rise and dance for His glory.

✓ Jesus laid aside His garment and laid aside His glory. He asks you to lay aside the weights and sins that hinder you from running this race. Lay aside the "I cannots!" Lay aside the "if onlys" that haunt your thought life every day. Let us follow our Master in laying aside an agenda for our glory and live the rest of our life for His glory!

✓ Jesus girded Himself with a servant's towel and took the form of a servant and became a Man. Let us gird ourselves with the armor of God. Let us follow His example and become His servant. If our Master calls us into a ministry of dance, let us not fear but let us do whatever He asks of us.

✓ Jesus began to wash the disciples' feet, even the one who He knew would betray Him. He continues to cleanse us from our sins. Let us follow our Master and humble ourselves and care for the Body of Christ in a way that pleases the Lord. We should even care for the ones who hurt us and maybe aren't what we think they should be. And when we dance for Him, let us proclaim loudly that we have experienced His cleansing power. We are sinners saved by grace!

By following Jesus' example, you are keeping the little foxes from ruining the vineyard. You can never go wrong by imitating your Master! When the world looks at you, may they see the serving heart of Jesus.

Therefore be imitators of God—copy Him and follow His example—as well-beloved children (imitate their father). (Ephesians 5:1 AMP)

Chapter 15
Dancing for Joy

You are about to embark upon one of the most exciting times in your life. We've talked much about some difficulties that may arise, but the joyful times far outweigh the trying times. You will be learning so many valuable eternal lessons as you let go and let God have His way in your life and dance ministry. One of the first lessons you will learn is that the Holy Spirit is the ultimate worship leader.

For we are the true circumcision, who worship in the Spirit of God and glory in Christ Jesus and put no confidence in the flesh. (Philippians 3:3)

He is the One who has orchestrated worship. He lives inside us and teaches us. It doesn't take long before we realize that we cannot make worship happen, but must become totally and completely abandoned to Him. He leads. We follow. No matter how many years we have led in a dance ministry, we must depend upon Jesus just as if it were our first dance together.

To keep your dance ministry dancing for joy you need each dancer to have these biblical characteristics in their personal lives. These attributes will help everyone have happy feet.

Going the Extra Mile

And if anyone forces you to go one mile, go with him two [miles]. (Matthew 5:41 AMP)

121

Many Christians do not have light on going the extra mile with our brothers and sisters-in-Christ. This is a deeper walk with Christ. It requires maturity and growth in the Lord. God is well pleased with a ministry that implements this biblical principle. Here are some helps to assure that you are going the extra mile with your dance partners:

✓ Don't feed on unloving thoughts about any dance member.

✓ Don't talk negatively about another dance member.

✓ Believe the best about each of the members of your team.

✓ Pray God's richest blessings upon each member of the dance team.

✓ Honor each member with words of affirmation.

✓ If you know a dance member is having a difficult time, invite them to your home and get to know them better.

✓ Always become part of the solution and never part of a problem that your dance ministry may be having.

Bridge Builder

There is a saying that goes like this—Without bridges the best-built roads would lead nowhere. The church today is full of too many wall builders and not enough bridge builders. Someone must be like Jesus and build a bridge. He built one with two pieces of wood and three rusty nails so that we could go to Heaven. This is one of the greatest secrets to a Spirit-filled ministry. It is a lost art in our society, but you can begin now by building bridges in the relationships between people in your dance ministry. Here are a few simple suggestions.

- ✓ Don't have a high opinion of your opinion. Removing a high opinion from your heart will help you build a bridge. You will be amazed, but it works every single time. May God give you the grace and courage to lay your "important" opinions at the foot of the Cross, so your dance ministry may be unified and go forward for the kingdom of God.

  For by the grace (unmerited favor of God) given to me I warn every one among you not to estimate and think of himself more highly than he ought—not to have an exaggerated opinion of his own importance; but to rate his ability with sober judgment, each according to the degree of faith apportioned by God to him. (Romans 12:3 AMP)

- ✓ When others are building walls with unkind words, you build a bridge with words of edification and affirmation.

- ✓ Be especially kind to those who are unkind to you. God will bless you for being a bridge builder. He will open doors for you that otherwise would have been shut. Bridge builders have accomplished great things for the Kingdom of God.

Shining Stars

And the teachers and those who are wise shall shine like the brightness of the firmament; and those who turn many to righteousness (to uprightness and right standing with God) [shall give forth light] like the stars for ever and ever." (Daniel 12:3 AMP)

The dance ministry that has dancers who are shining stars will find that they light the way wherever they go. The world is a dark place, but shining stars shine in the midst of the darkness. They brighten everyone days by allowing God's love to blaze through them. Here are few ways the shining stars stand out:

✓ They shine with a great attitude no matter what their circumstances.

✓ They shine with thankfulness.

✓ They have a gigantic servant's heart.

✓ They walk in love. They aren't moody.

✓ They esteem others above themselves.

The shining stars have discovered that there's only one way to spell joy!

Jesus first!
Others second!
Yourself last!

Team Player

We've often heard the little saying that "team" does not have an "I" in it! For a dance ministry to be the very best for Jesus that it can be, everyone should be a team player. This means if one dancer receives more credit or glory, it does not cause jealousy or envy in any other the other dancers. They recognize that they are all playing on the same team. This is an advanced step in the Christian life. Many novices stumble here. It's time to grow up and not remain a babe in Christ. Be a team player and cheer on the other dance team members and watch God give the increase.

Rare Treasure

A dance ministry must somehow unify under the Bloodstained banner and be one heartbeat. There is no substitute for unity. Unity in a ministry makes all the difference between success and failure. It is an essential factor, which makes your dance ministry invincible. For unity to take place outwardly, miracles must take place inwardly. Humility replaces pride. Loving affirmation replaces competition. Love replaces jealousy. Dancers can no longer be full of themselves because they know if they are there is no room for the Holy Spirit of God. So, they allow God to discipline them and deal with them about their nature faults, and as He prunes and removes those sometimes hidden weaknesses, He replaces them with His precious Holy Spirit. Oh, may each dancer be a rare treasure for the Master.

Helping Hand

One would think that all dance ministries would be concerned about are dancing feet, but to experience excellence in a dance ministry there must be many helping hands—those who possibly dance, but work behind the scenes, too. All dancers should have the heart of a servant. They should strive to out-serve one another. Questions they should ask their worship leader are ...

✓ How can I help?

✓ How can I lighten your load?

✓ Is there anything I can do to help?

✓ Do you need anything right now?

✓ How can I be a blessing to you?

✓ Is there anything that you can delegate to the dance team so you aren't under such a load?

✓ Does the platform need clearing before the meeting or put back together after the meeting?

✓ Does any equipment need to be brought in?

✓ What job do you want me responsible for?

Many times people don't help simply because they don't see they are needed. Make yourself available. Go out of the way to reassure your leaders that there is no job too humble for your helping hands.

For even the Son of man came not to have service rendered to Him, but to serve, and to give His life as a ransom for (instead of) man. (Mark 10:45 AMP)

Chapter 16
One Dance at a Time

When it comes to a dance ministry the dancer must always remember it's not how much you know, but it's whom you know. As you dance for the Lord, people will begin to see the Lord. Some are seeing Him for the very first time. Others may experience seeing a clearer vision of Him. That's what a consecrated dance ministry is all about—seeing Him.

In the year that King Uzziah died, (in a vision) I saw the Lord sitting upon a throne high and lifted up, and the skirts of His train filled the (most holy part of the) temple. (Isaiah 6:1 AMP)

Inferiority is an Enemy

Inferiority magnifies my lack. Inferiority is an enemy of the Cross. It will hinder you from doing God's will if you let it. The Bible is full of men and women that God called, who felt inferior. Some even argued with God that He couldn't really want to use them. Maybe you are in that number. You must remember to trust your wise Heavenly Father and take your dance ministry one dance at a time. You cannot trust your feelings, but you can trust the One who has called you into this exciting adventure. Your God has an uncanny way of taking ordinary people and using them to do extraordinary feats.

Moses

And Moses said to the Lord, O Lord, I am not eloquent or a man of words, neither before nor since You have spoken to Your servant; for I am slow of speech, and have a heavy and awkward tongue. And the Lord said to him, Who has made man's mouth? Or who makes the dumb, or deaf, or the seeing, or the blind? Is it not I, the Lord? Now therefore go, and I will be with your mouth, and will teach you what you shall say. (Exodus 4:10-12 AMP)

The God of Moses is your God, too. If He has called you into this ministry, He will equip you. He will not fail you. Remember, take it one dance at a time.

Gideon

Gideon said to Him, Oh, Lord, how can I deliver Israel? Behold, my clan is the poorest in Manasseh, and I am the least in my father's house. The Lord said to him, Surely I will be with you and you shall smite the Midianites as one man." (Judges 6:15-16 AMP)

The God of Gideon is your God, too. Maybe you are scarred from past hurts. Possibly you weren't raised in a Christian home and you think someone else would do a better job and be more qualified. The fact of the matter is this—GOD HAS CALLED YOU! And if God called you, He will not fail you. Remember our motto, one dance at a time!

Isaiah

Then said I, Woe is me! For I am undone and ruined, because I am a man of unclean lips, and dwell in the midst of people of unclean lips; for my eyes have seen the King, the Lord of hosts!" (Isaiah 6:5 AMP)

The God of the mighty prophet Isaiah is your God, too. It might be that you don't feel worthy to fulfill this call that God has placed on your life. Doubts may plague you. Fears may haunt you. Isaiah felt that way, but then he had an encounter that changed his perspective.

Then flew one of the seraphim (heavenly beings) to me, having a live coal in his hand which he had taken with tongs from off the altar; and with it he touched my mouth and said, Lo, this has touched your lips; your iniquity and guilt are taken away, and your sin is completely atoned for and forgiven. Also I heard the voice of the Lord saying, Whom shall I send and who will go for Us? Than I said I, Here am I; send me. And He said, Go, and tell this people." (Isaiah 6:6-9 AMP)

Isaiah was not the same after he had this encounter with his holy God. God is our holy King and has given us His Holy Spirit to clean us up. The Holy Spirit was given to God's people to make them more holy. His Spirit will give you the strength to go forth and do what He has called you to do. Go forth in the power of His resurrection. Faithful is He who called you.

Faithful is He Who is calling you (to Himself) and utterly trustworthy, and He will also do it (that is, fulfill His call by hallowing and keeping you). (1 Thessalonians 5:24 AMP)

Abraham

When Abram was 99 years old, the Lord appeared to him, and said, I am the Almighty God; walk and live habitually before Me, and be perfect—blameless, whole-hearted, complete. And God said to Abraham, As for Sarai your wife, you shall not call her name Sarai, but Sarah (princess) her name shall be. And I will bless her, and give you a son also of her; yes, I will bless her, and she shall be

129

*a mother of nations; kings of peoples shall come from her.
Then Abraham fell on his face and laughed." (Genesis
17:1,15-17 AMP)*

Abraham was noted as being a friend of God. Yet
when God told him that He was going to give him a son, he
fell on his face and laughed. Maybe you feel like that as
God is calling you into a dance ministry. Maybe you feel
you are too old just as Abraham felt. God proved to
Abraham that He kept His Word. God will keep His Word
to you, too. So many times we doubt God instead of
doubting our doubts. Today let's change that nasty habit.
Let's doubt our doubts and believe our true and mighty
God, who has never failed us and never will. If He has
called you to do something, He will be with you each step
of the way. He will teach you and guide you. Great is His
faithfulness. He will be with you one dance at a time. The
God of Abraham is your God, too. Now if that's doesn't
give you something to dance about, nothing will.
Hallelujah!

Chapter 17
Lord of the Dance

There is a wonderful hymn written by Sydney B. Carter in 1963. The lyrics are powerful and tell a wonderful story.

Lord of the Dance

"I danced in the morning when the world was begun,
And I danced on the moon and the stars and the sun,
And I came down from Heaven and I danced on the earth,
At Bethlehem I had my birth.

I danced for the scribe and the Pharisee,
But they would not dance and they would not follow me;
I danced for the fishermen, for James and John;
They came to me and the dance went on.

I danced on the Sabbath when I cured the lame,
The holy people said it was a shame;
They whipped and they stripped and they hung me high;
And they left me there on a cross to die.

I danced on a Friday and the sky turned black;
It's hard to dance with the devil on your back;
They buried my body and they thought I'd gone,
But I am the dance and I still go on.

They cut me down and I leapt up high,
I am the life that will never ever die;
I'll live in you if you'll live in me;

131

I am the Lord of the Dance, said he.

Dance, then, wherever you may be;
I am the Lord of the Dance, said he.
And I'll lead you all wherever you may be,
And I'll lead you all in the dance said he."[1]

Can't you sense the victory in these profound lyrics? That's what the Lord of the Dance wants to do in your life and ministry! He longs to bring victory to you personally. Victories that only He can bring. There will be times you may not feel like dancing, but we must remember that we do not dance by feelings. We dance by faith. In fact, we may experience greater victories when we dance for Him when we don't feel like it because we are obeying the Word of God.

Though the fig tree should not blossom, and there be no fruit on the vines, though the yield of the olive should fail, and the fields produce no food, though the flock should be cut off from the fold, and there be no cattle in the stalls, yet I will exult in the Lord, I will rejoice in the God of my salvation. The Lord God is my strength, and He has made my feet like hinds' feet, and makes me walk on my high places." (Habakkuk 3:17-19)

There is power in praise. There is a supernatural anointing when we begin to worship, rejoice, dance and sing, especially when our outward circumstances are taxing. God loves when we rely upon Him. He loves to prove Himself strong in our behalf. No matter how bleak her situation, a true minister of dance will continue to

---

[1] Copyright 1963 Stainer & Bell Ltd. London, England

worship. You are called to be that true minister of dance! Continue to lead others into His glorious Presence. You can never out give the Giver. In the beginning of a dance ministry, people may be tempted to think that they are giving God something in return, but as they dance in the Spirit and experience His Divine Presence, they realize that one can never out give the Lord. He never stops giving! He never stops blessing! He does grow sweeter as the years go by!

God's Fingerprints

As you fall in love with the Lord of the Dance and begin your dance ministry, you will begin to see God's fingerprints on many of the doors the Lord opens for you. It can be as simple as God answering the prayers of the dance team or some miraculous way that God has made provision for your dance ministry's needs. Always be sensitive to seeing with the eyes of your soul to what God is trying to teach you and the dance team. Share openly with the dance ministry that God has put them together with His fingerprints being evident. This will build your faith and give your ministry a firm foundation as time passes. And when the storms come, and they will, your ministry will be built upon the Rock! No matter how strong the winds are, your ministry will stand.

You are on a sacred journey. The Lord of the Dance has entrusted you with a holy call, which will have a profound impact on the precious souls He brings across your path. It is vital that He can trust you. Remember to always give the glory and the honor to the King. This simple teaching will keep you from becoming a stumbling block to the Body of Christ. Always be about the King's business, and never exalt yourself in the King's presence. Your emphasis is always the King!

Do not claim honor in the presence of the king. (Proverbs 25:6)

False Worship

As we study the Bible, we soon discover that Satan has a counterfeit for everything that God has ordained for us. This is also true about worship. We are warned in the Old Testament about false worship. The first commandment tells us that we are to only worship the one true God.

You shall have no other gods before or besides Me. (Exodus 20:3 AMP)

God commands that we do not worship other gods, which is a form of idolatry. May we never worship our dance ministry more than we worship the Lord of the Dance. We must always keep our priorities straight so that we are pleasing the Lord. Take time to get quiet before the Lord and allow Him to totally and completely sanctify your heart and motives.

Most earnest Christians do not struggle with the false worship of idolatry in their lives, but the Lord has another form of false worship that He warns us about in His Word.

This people draw near Me with their mouth and honor Me with their lips, but their heart holds off and is far away from Me; Uselessly do they worship Me, for they teach as doctrines the commands of men." (Matthew 15:8-9 AMP)

Going through the motions and not worshipping from the heart is another form of false worship that a dance ministry must guard against. We must eat from the Tree of Life every day and keep our personal relationship with Jesus fresh and vibrant. Formalism and ritual in worship does great damage to the Church of Jesus Christ! Don't allow it in your life or ministry. Repent of any wrong attitude of your heart as quickly as the Lord reveals it to you. This will keep your life and dance ministry renewed and anointed.

Another form of false worship that offends the Lord of the Dance is when worship is married to hypocrisy.

Samuel said, Has the Lord as great delight in burnt offerings and sacrifices, as in obeying the voice of the Lord? Behold, to obey is better than to sacrifice, and to hearken than the fat of rams. (I Samuel 15:22 AMP)

Thus says the Lord of hosts, the God of Israel: Add your burnt offerings to your sacrifices, and eat the flesh [if you will. It will avail you nothing]. For in the day that I brought them out of the land of Egypt, I did not speak to your fathers or command them concerning burnt offerings or sacrifices. But this thing I did command them: Listen to and obey My voice, and I will be your God, and you shall be My people; and walk in the whole way that I command you, that it may be well with you. But they would not listen and obey, or bend their ear to Me, but followed the counsels and the stubborn promptings of their own evil hearts and minds, and they turned their back and went in reverse instead of forward. (Jeremiah 7:21-24 AMP)

Sacrifice and offering You do not desire, nor have You delight in them; You have given me capacity to hear and obey (Your law, a more valuable service then) burnt and sin offerings which You do not require. Then said I, Lo, I come; in the volume of the book it is written of me, I delight to do Your will, O my God; yes, Your law is within my heart. I have proclaimed glad tidings of righteousness in the great assembly—tidings of uprightness and right standing with God. Lo, I have not restrained my lips, as You know, O Lord. I have not concealed Your righteous-

ness with my heart; I have proclaimed Your faithfulness and Your salvation; I have not hid away Your steadfast love and Your truth from the great assembly. (Psalm 40: 6-10 AMP)

What a testimony there is in a clean life. In this present evil world we live in, won't you be a light for Jesus? As you do, you will discover the power of holiness that can break the enemy's back. Sin will not have dominion over you. Be clean for Jesus.

Therefore do not let sin reign in your mortal body that you should obey its lusts, and do not go on presenting the members of your body to sin as instruments of unrighteousness; but present yourselves to God as those alive from the dead, and our members as instruments of righteousness to God. For sin shall not be master over you, for you are not under law, but under grace. (Romans 6:12-14)

There is something to be said for ministers and ministries that finish the race strong. Their testimony lives long after they are gone. Even though they are dead, yet they speak. Oh, may your life and ministry be clean for Jesus and bring much honor to the Lord of the Dance so that long after you are gone, you will have left footprints in the souls of those you've ministered to.

...though he is dead, he still speaks." (Hebrews 11:4)

Chapter 18
A Dance for All Seasons

We have covered so much territory in our time together. My prayer for you is that you will see that it doesn't matter what your age, race or economic background—God can use you. I have discovered over and over again that if you will find your "mess" you will find the ministry God has for you. Go back to the place where Jesus found you. There are many others who are hurting in that same place. They are looking for a way out, and you know the way out! Jesus led you out so you can lead others out. Oh, don't believe the lies of the enemy that whisper, "You are too old. You are too young. You aren't smart enough. You aren't rich enough. You aren't educated enough." Just look at what God has done for you. He has saved you. He has delivered you. He has healed your broken heart. The world is full of lost souls bound by the enemy's chains, and their hearts are broken. The Lord wants to use you to make a difference in their lives. I'm fully aware of what the enemy is telling you, "You don't know my neighborhood! You don't know my situation!" That's true, I may not know, but Jesus knows and nothing is impossible with Him. It is His will to come to your neighborhood. It is His will to come to your situation. But Jesus needs someone who will say, "Here am I, Lord! Send me!" Oh, let Jesus use you for one soul at a time. Jesus will lead you and give you a dance for whatever season people are facing in their lives. This is exactly what happened to me.

Dance of Hope

After I had ministered in dance in a church in Mississippi, a twenty-two-year-old young lady came up to me. She was deeply moved by my dance, and shared how her pastor's son had been killed in a tragic automobile accident on the first day of school in 2004. She had danced for the Lord the Sunday before the accident, and the pastor's son had commented on how it had ministered to him. She was so devastated that she had not danced for the Lord since his death. After she saw me dance, hope was resurrected on the inside of her. I could have listened to the devil's lies telling me that a middle-aged woman dancing for Jesus wouldn't bless a young person, but I didn't. I obeyed the Lord. He called me to dance, and through my obedience this young lady was delivered from her grief and hopelessness. After she shared her painful story, I took the time to choreograph a piece of music for her to dance to. She told me that she was now ready to dance for the Lord again. When we were finished, we embraced and she thanked me for helping her through a very difficult place. I knew as she was walking away that God had orchestrated our meeting. And, my dear friend, God has some divine orchestration that He wants to do in your life. Will you surrender and obey the call to bloom wherever you are planted? You won't regret a mile!

A Dancer's Spiritual Needs

A spiritual dancer has spiritual needs that must be met to enable the dancer to have a dance for all seasons. These spiritual needs cannot be stressed enough.

Spiritual dancers are worshippers. Worship is based on an intimate relationship with Jesus. Dancers must be sure that they engage in a personal walk with Him! This helps them to be in tune and know what type of dance to perform. God may have a dance team enter a church where there is great division. The dancers may have been practicing a praise and worship dance long and hard, but as the dancers are seeking the Lord in prayer, God makes it very real to them that this church needs an intercessory dance to break strongholds. This is the dance for that season! Only a close intimate relationship with Jesus would reveal this. Whatever a dancer may think their greatest need is today, their greatest need is more of Jesus! Don't ever neglect Him!

Spiritual dancers no longer follow their personal agenda. They are always about their Father's business and don't have time to waste on fleshly ambitions. They have been well trained in the Master's army. They have learned to submit to authority. Their struggles with submission have ended and are honored to be called are servants of the Lord. They realize how short life really is and the importance of being led by the Spirit.

Spiritual dancers develop from the inside out. Inwardly they are growing and learning how to walk in the Spirit. The Spirit of God is the dancer's greatest resource. The Spirit will lead you into all truth and teach you to dance.

Spiritual dancers cultivate a quiet heart. They know how to still their soul so they can hear the voice of their Master. It is essential that spiritual dancers find space to breathe and time to think. Remember, God often speaks in a still small voice.

Surely I have calmed and quieted my soul, like a weaned child with his mother; like a weaned child is my soul within me (ceased from fretting). (Psalm 131:2 AMP)

Spiritual dancers have a balanced life. They do not thrive on activity overload that is so prevalent in our day and age. They constantly keep the main thing the main thing! They major on the major and minor on the minors. This way they are free to minister with great freedom. They realize that many times God speaks through stillness and when a dancer's life is cluttered with too much "stuff," she suffers. The people she is called to minister to suffer. Oh, let 's lay aside the weights that so easily beset us!

Therefore then, since we are surrounded by so great a cloud of witnesses (who have borne testimony of the Truth), let us strip off and throw aside every encumbrance – unnecessary weight – and that sin which so readily (deftly and cleverly) clings and entangles us, and let us run with patient endurance and steady and active persistence the appointed course of the race that is set before us, looking away (from all that will distract) to Jesus, Who is the Leader and the Source of our faith (giving the first incentive for our belief) and is also its Finisher, (bringing it to maturity and perfection). He, for the joy (of obtaining the prize) that was set before Him, endured the cross, despising and ignoring the shame, and is now seated at the right hand of the throne of God. (Hebrews 12:1-2 AMP)

Spiritual dancers keep their eyes upon Jesus and allow Him to change them from glory to glory.

And all of us, as with unveiled face, (because we) continued to behold (in the Word of God) as in a mirror the glory of the Lord, are constantly being transfigured into His very own image in ever increasing splendor and from one degree of glory to another; (for this comes) from the Lord (Who is) the Spirit. (2 Corinthians 3:18 AMP)

Chapter 19
Heavenly Dance

As you enter into intimate worship with the Bridegroom of your soul, you will discover that worship lasts for all eternity. Worship begins in this life by catching a glimpse of Jesus with the eyes of your soul! This vision of Jesus causes you to march to the beat of a different drum. Your life is changed forever. If this was all that happened it would be enough, but it doesn't stop there. Worship lasts for all eternity. Even when we arrive in Heaven we will worship. In the Book of Revelation we are given a window to peek through and see what is taking place in heaven right now.

After this I looked and a vast host appeared which no one could count, (gathered out) of every nation, from all tribes and peoples and languages. These stood before the throne and before the Lamb; they were attired in white robes, with palm branches in their hands. In loud voice they cried, saying, (Our) salvation is due to our God Who is seated on the throne, and to the Lamb – to Them (we owe our) deliverance! And all the angels were standing round the throne and round the elders (of the heavenly Sanhedrin) and the four living creatures, and they fell prostrate before the throne and worshipped God. Amen! (So be it!) they cried. Blessing and glory and majesty and splendor and wisdom and thanks and honor and power and might (be ascribed) to our God to the ages and ages—forever and ever, throughout the eternities of the eternities! Amen! (So be it!) Then, addressing me, one of the elders (of the heavenly Sanhedrin) said, Who are these (people) clothed

*in the long white robes? And from where have they come? I
replied, Sir, you know. And he said to me, These are they
who have come out of the great tribulation (persecution),
and have washed their robes and made them white in the
blood of the Lamb. For this reason they are (now) before
the (very) throne of God, and serve Him day and night in
His (temple) sanctuary; and He Who is sitting upon the
throne will protect and spread His tabernacle over and
shelter them with His Presence. They shall hunger no more,
neither thirst any more, neither shall the sun smite them,
nor any scorching heat. For the Lamb Who is in the midst
of the throne will be their Shepherd, and He will guide
them to the springs of the waters of Life; and God will wipe
every tear away from their eyes. (Revelation 7:9-17 AMP)*

Oh, what precious promises! Did you see this
priceless picture? The saints of God were attired in white
robes (their dance costume), and they held palm branches
in their hands (their dance props). They began to worship
the Lord. The anointing fell so strongly as they worshipped
that the elders of the heavenly Sanhedrin fell prostrate
before the throne and worshipped God. Heaven is full of
worship!

Some of you have come out of great persecution.
You have deep scars from your past, but now the Blood of
the Lamb has washed you whiter than freshly fallen snow.
You have been forgiven much and you in return love much.
The words of Jesus in the Gospel of Luke put it this way.

*Wherefore I say unto thee, her sins, which are
many, are forgiven; for she loved much: but to whom little
is forgiven, the same loveth little. (Luke 7:47 KJV)*

No longer should the past haunt you with thoughts
of condemnation. Jesus has forgiven you much, which
causes you to love Him much in return. Out of that love
comes an intimate worship experience. You have been

called to dance. Jesus has given you this "Heavenly Dance" to bless the Body of Christ. He longs to come to others the way He has come to you. He desires to use you to help heal others the way He has healed you. Dance for Jesus! Dance for mighty deliverances in His Name! As you do He will be coming to your heart and revealing Himself more and more to you.

Back in the mid-forties, a forty-year-old alcoholic woman from Charles City, Iowa, took a trip to Metropolis, Illinois, to see her brother. She planned to cross the border into Kentucky and pick up some moonshine. She was a bootlegger and planned on bringing the alcohol home to sell. When she arrived at her brother's house, he invited her to some revival meetings that his church was having. She had never been to church in her life, not even as a little girl. She had no desire to go, but she loved her brother and just to please him she agreed to go. When she arrived at the meeting, she sat on the back pew. The music started and people began to dance before the Lord. She had never seen anything like it in her entire life. After a while the minister stood and began to preach. Hot tears began to fall down her cheeks. The minister invited all who wanted to start a new life in Christ to come forward. Somehow she had enough courage to stand and walk down that aisle and knelt at an old-fashioned altar. Many of the deaconesses of the church gathered around her. Some stood and others knelt beside her. She began to repent of her sins. As she was repenting, some of the ladies began to shout and dance around her. She had never been exposed to anything like this before in her life. She wept before the Lord as the Holy Spirit brought different sins to her mind. As the Lord revealed these sins she promptly told the Lord how sorry she was. As the women were praising and dancing in the Holy Ghost, this dear woman sensed a demonic stronghold of alcoholism leave her body. After several hours she stood to her feet a new woman in Christ. She never went to Kentucky to pick up the moonshine. She went back to

Charles City, Iowa, and began telling everyone she knew that Jesus had saved her and delivered her from alcoholism. She never touched another drop of alcohol and lived to be ninety-two years old. Something happened in that revival meeting in Metropolis, Illinois. Godly deaconesses obeying the Spirit in a dance destroyed the powers of darkness. The deliverance God brought that night has affected generations after her. She could have left a legacy of alcoholism and abuse, but instead left a legacy of victory over a curse that had kept her family bound for generations. Little did that dear woman know that her decision to follow Christ would affect generations that followed her, but it did; because of her testimony many of her family members follow Christ yet to this day. For many years this same lady pastored a church in her poor neighborhood. On numerous occasions hopeless alcoholics were brought to the services. This same lady who was once bound by the same demons that these trapped souls were, would pray and dance over them until deliverance came. Little did those deaconesses in Metropolis know that by their obedience to the Lord they, too, were bringing precious victories to many families they would never meet so desperately needing a touch from the Lord.

This might be your experience, too. You may never know until you get to Heaven what eternal benefit your dance has brought to someone else. Your obeying the Lord in your dance ministry may affect future generations.

Don't let the enemy steal your joy. Don't let him torment you with condemning thoughts. Don't let him plague you with inferior thoughts. Just obey the Lord and dance. The joy of the Lord is your strength. The church needs you to walk in your Levitical Call. Future generations need your help. Keep your eyes on Jesus and your hand on the plow. Don't look back. Go forward in Jesus' Name!

Jesus said to him, No one who puts his hand to the plow and looks back (to the things behind) is fit for the kingdom of God. (Luke 9:62 AMP)

Jesus will equip you. He isn't looking for great ability, but He is looking for availability. Avail yourself to Him. He has called you. He will equip you. He will not fail you.

Faithful is he that calleth you, who also will do it. (I Thessalonians 5:24 KJV)

Go forth and celebrate Jesus, one dance at a time!

Chapter 20
Dance Resources

To become an effective dance ministry, you need to take time to learn and always attempt to sharpen your skills. You may not be able to attend a conference or seminar, but you can purchase a DVD or VHS and learn in the privacy of your own living room. You can also play a DVD or VHS for the entire dance team to learn new songs and techniques. There are some workshop ministries that will come to your church and host a banner or dance seminar for a minimal fee. Be creative and let the Lord lead you into the direction that He would have you go. Below is a list of dance resources that can help you dance for the Lord with confidence.

Resource List for Dancewear

The following is a list of places where you can purchase dance shoes, dancewear, undergarments and accessories.

The Movement Connection
24118 Lorain Road
North Olmsted, OH 44070
Phone (440) 779-0500
Fax (440) 779-1077
Toll Free: (877) 326-2300
sales@movementconnection.com

His Majesty's Dancewear
1860 South Street. Rt. 42
Lebanon, OH 45036
(888) 725-4459
(Call to receive a catalog)

The Ballet Barre
401 East Kennedy Street
Spartanburg, SC 29302
(866) 325-7388
www.praise-dancewear.com

The Hosiery Stop
3825 Main Street
College Park, GA 30337
(404) 768-0076
www.hosierystop.com

Discount Dancewear & Praise Apparel
431 Stacy Weaver Drive
Fayetteville, NC 28311
Phone (877) 650-5030
Fax (910) 482-3508
www.discountdanceapparel.com

Dance Distributors
(800) 333-2326
www.dancedistributors.com

Praise Dancewear & Accessories
1023 East 161st Place
South Holland, IL 60473
(773) 239-6691
www.geocities.com/grantdesigns1/kingdomgarments

Sure Foundation Shape Wear
428 George Avenue
Selfridge, MI 48045
(586) 468-4213

**Resource List for Worship Props
(Streamers, Banners, Scarves, Banners, Ribbons,
Hoops and Tambourines)**

Signs of God Banners
P.O. Box 42221
Charleston, SC 20423
(843) 552-7150
www.signsofgodbanners.com

Praise Banners
1-800-Banners
www.praisebanners.com

The Praise Props Shoppe
610 Pleasant Valley Road
New Ringgold, PA 17960
(570) 943-3149
www.praisepropsshoppe.tripod.com/index

Kingdom Celebration
www.kingdomcelebration.com

Total Praise Design
www.worship-dance.com

Humble Heart Ministries
P.O. Box 958333
Hoffman Estates, IL 60195-8333
Phone (847) 755-1454
Fax (847) 839-1426
www.humble-heart.com

Out of our Mind Banners
Toowoomba, QLD 4350
Australia
61-7-4638-3890
www.worshipbanners.org

**Resource List for Dance Ministry Classes,
Seminars and Workshops**

Chenaniah Studio
For the Ministering Arts
2020 Shipley Drive Suite A 1
Salisbury, MD 21801
www.chenaniahstudio.com
(410) 546-2165

Chenaniah Praise Dancers
Dancing with Authority Conference
P.O. Box 243741
Boynton Beach, FL 33424
www.chenaniah.org/home

Karitos
25-B N. Belmont Avenue
Arlington Heights, IL 60004
www.karitos.com
(847) 749-1284
(630) 243-8127

Joy Ministry
P.O. Box 4561
Fayetteville, AR 72702
(479) 582-1855
www.joyministry.com

Gospel Music Ministries International
P.O. Box 1782
Pittsburgh, PA 15230
www.bobbyfulton.com

Christian Assembly
4099 Karl Road
Columbus, OH 43224
Phone (614) 261-8440
Fax (614) 261-8732
www.exaltationohio.com

Dancing for Him
8 Good Hope Road
Lawrenceburg, TN 38484
Phone (931) 829-2705
www.dancingforhim.com

Moved by the Spirit
Sacred Dance Ministry
Ms. Angel Simmons
Phone (773) 737-6909

McClean Bible Church
Heather Brennan
P.O. Box 9300
McClean, VA 22102
Phone (703) 770-2981
www.mcleanbible.org

Pershay Dance Ministry Corporation
219-26 138 Road
Laurelton, NY 11413
Phone (718) 749-7957
Fax (212) 454-0106
www.pershaywardance4u.com

School of Dance
P.O. Box 621367
Littleton, CO 80162-1367
Phone (303) 470-5856
www.magnifythelord.org

Son Life Dance Company
1203 Vandalia
Collinsville, IL 62234
(618) 345-4249

Alfred Street Baptist Church
301 S. Alfred Street
Alexandria, VA 22314
Phone (703) 683-2222
Fax (703) 683-1718
www.danceministry.net

Glory Dance Ministries
P.O. 10373
Wilmington, NC 28404
(910) 452-0588
www.glorydance.com

Karar Dance Ministry Workshop
632 West Main Street
Charlottesville, VA 22903
www.transminfbc.org

Ministry in Motion
15003 Joy Road
Detroit, MI 48228
LaShonya Thomas
(313) 534-8796

One Chord Arts' Resources
P. O. Box 1451
Simpsonville, SC 29681
www.onechord.org

World Shaker Dancers
1155 Terrace Street
Muskegon, MI 49442
Minister Leya Elijah Oliver
Artisticdiva78@aol.com
(231) 728-3807

Praise Him with Dance
3801 Hwy. 293 Suites B-D
Kennesaw, GA 30144
(770) 974-8653
phwd@mindspring.com

Resource List for Dance-Mentoring Online

Pastor Pamela Rutherford-Hardy
Set Free Evangelistic Ministries
P.O. Box 568
Reynoldsburg, OH 43068
Phone (214) 402-9647
Fax (614) 863-8732
www.worshipdance.org

Resource List for Dance Ministry Magazine

Dance Spirit
P.O. 2041
Marion, OH 43306-2141

Resource List for Dance Ministry Videos

Chosen Generation Volume 1 Worship
Chosen Generation Volume 2 Prophesy
P.O. Box 1508
Hamilton, AL 35570
(800) 345-2736
www.karenwheaton.com

Christian Ministry Resource
A Tabernacle of Praise – Ladies' Dance - DVD
A Tabernacle of Praise – As Miriam Did – Tambourines - DVD
A Tabernacle of Praise – Jehovah Nissi – Flags – DVD
A Tabernacle of Praise – Mens' Dance - DVD
Called to Dance – DVD & VHS
Creative Worship – DVD & VHS
Dance Into Battle – VHS

Dance! Dance! Dance! – DVD & VHS
Let's Dance – VHS
Dancing Word – Miriam & Mary - VHS
I Lift Your Name on High – DVD
Teach Your Feet – 1 – Basic Dance Combinations - VHS
Teach Your Feet - 2 – Basic Dance Combinations –VHS
Expressive Sign – DVD
Choreography Tips & Techniques – DVD
Devotional Dance Workshop – DVD
Davidic Dance – DVD
Expressive Worship/Prophetic Dance – DVD & VHS
Glorious – DVD
Now is the Time – VHS
Prophetic Dance Workshop – DVD & VHS
Stretch & Adoration – VHS
Biblical Basis for Dance – DVD

Warobics – DVD & VHS

Weapons of Warfare – Movements of Breakthrough – DVD
www.christianministryresource.com

Restored to Glory
Video Dance Clips
www.danceministry.com

Worship Steps
Glorious Video
Shackles Video
I Need Thee Video
Please Walk Beside Me Video
P.O. Box 664
Longview, WA 98632
www.worshipsteps.com

N'Him
Called to Dance Video
www.n-him.org

One Chord Arts' Resource Ministry
Heart of One Chord – DVD
Freedom in His Presence – DVD
The Blood – DVD
Praise Groove – DVD
Turning into Glory – DVD
Holy Hands Upraised – DVD
Touch of Grace – DVD
Praise & Worship in Motion – DVD
Intimate Dance to an Awesome God - DVD
P.O. Box 1451
Simpsonville, SC 29681
Phone (864) 906-7317
www.onechord.org

Chapter 21
Inspirational Dance Quotes

The Scripture God has given me for
Soaring Eagles Dance Ministry is ...

They will come and shout for joy on the heights of Zion: they will rejoice in the bounty of the Lord-the grain, the new wine and the olive oil, the young of the flocks and herds. They will be like a well-watered garden, and they will sorrow no more. Then the young women will dance and be glad, young men and old as well. I will turn their mourning into gladness; I will give them comfort and joy instead of sorrow. I will satisfy the priests with abundance, and my people will be filled with my bounty declares the Lord (Jeremiah 31:12-14 TNIV)

True worship always forgets itself. – Matt Redman

When in doubt...DANCE! – Anonymous

You can dance anywhere, even if only in your heart! – Anonymous

Dancers are the athletes of God! – Albert Einstein

Life is a dance from one stage to the next! – Anonymous

Dancing with the feet is one thing, but dancing with the heart is another! – Anonymous

*Behind each victory dance is along trail of suffering! –
Anonymous*

Dance for life! – Anonymous

*Dance as if there are only so many tomorrows! –
Anonymous*

*If dancing were any easier it would be called football! –
Anonymous*

*Dancers aren't made of their technique but of their
passion! – Anonymous*

*Thank God you are able to dance! Remember there are
those who cannot even walk! – Anonymous*

Dancing is like dreaming with your feet! – Constanze

Fly

Through the dance we learn
to become centered,
to find balance,
to fall,
to recover,
to risk,
to stretch,
to leap,
to soar,
and in some rare
and beautiful moments...
to fly!
- Rebecca Wright Phillips

*I don't want people who want to dance, I want people who
have to dance! - George Balanchine*

They sent forth their children as a flock; their little ones dance about. They sing to the music of the timbrel and lyre; they make merry to the sound of the pipe. They spend their years in prosperity and go down to the grave in peace.
(Job 21:11-13 TNIV)

Dance like no one is watching. Sing like no one is listening. Love like you have never had been hurt and live like it is Heaven on Earth. – Mark Twain

You turned my wailing into dancing; you removed my sackcloth and clothed me with joy, that my heart may sing your praises and not be silent. Lord my God, I will praise you forever. (Psalm 30:11-12 TNIV)

Dancing makes us kinder and happier more likely to love and be loved, less likely to go out and hurt ourselves.
-Unknown

There is a time for everything, and a season for every activity under the heavens: A time to weep and a time to laugh, a time to mourn and a time to dance.
(Ecclesiastes 3:1-4 TNIV)

The first question of value: Can they walk? Even more important, Can they dance?
-Unknown

If you speak, you should do so as one who speaks the very words of God. If you serve[Dance] you should do so with the strength God provides, so that in all things God may be praised through Jesus Christ. To him be the glory and the power for ever and ever. Amen! (1 Peter 4:11 TNIV)

Nobody cares if you can't dance well. Just get up and dance. Great dancers are not great because of their technique, they're great because of their passion.
-Martha Graham

Dance is the only art of which we ourselves are the stuff of which it is made. -Ted Shawn

A king can be judged by the state of dance during his reign.

You've Never Felt Pain Until You've Walked In A Dancer's Shoes."
-Unknown

Dancers are like instruments, like a piano the choreographer plays! – George Balanchine

Dance till the stars come down from the rafters. Dance, dance, dance till you drop! – W.H. Auden

Conclusion

Dancing for God After Fifty has propelled me to a place of seeking to understand the meaning of dance in worship. I know for a fact that Satan continues to counterfeit anything that is good and of God. Therefore, he works overtime contaminating that which brings God the Greatest Joy – praise and worship!

Judith Rock makes this point explicit in *Biblical Criteria in Modern Dance: Modern Dance as a Prophetic Form*. Rock states, "It is becoming more understood as we begin to realize that our society is being led by a force that dehumanizes humans, made in the image of God, to nothing more than super-species or animals. A society that tries to force us to reduce conscience to nothing more than instinct, love to sex only, the personal to the impersonal, order to disorder, and finally, humanity to inhumanity. As a Christian modern dancer, I proclaim, a prophetic modern dance that tells us something about how it is to be human."

This is our call in the church as a dancer for God at any age. We are to proclaim righteousness in the creativity that has been granted us for the edification of God's kingdom. As we soar in the ministry of dance we shall always endeavor to keep our eyes on the One who is really the wind beneath our wings. Dance! Soar! Fly!

About the Author

Pastor Roberts is a native of Monticello, Mississippi, and an alumna of Alcorn State University, Lorman, Mississippi, and the Interdenominational Theological Center, Atlanta, Georgia. She earned a Master of Divinity specializing in Psychology. She was awarded a Doctorate of Humanities from the Panama City Theological Seminary, Panama City, Florida. She is presently pursuing a Doctorate of Homiletics at Interdenominational Theological Center, Atlanta, Georgia. Following her ordination from the Church of God in Christ, Pastor Roberts completed Clinical Pastoral Educational at Clinical Memorial Hospital, Atlanta, Georgia, after which she served as chaplain for female offenders for Atlanta Advancement Center.

Commissioned as an Army Chaplain in January 1985, Pastor Roberts' first duty station was Fort Rucker, Alabama, where she served as chaplain for the hospital and 1–13th Aviation Battalion. Subsequent assignments include Nurnburg, Germany, Saudi Arabia (Desert Storm), Fort Stewart and Fort Gordon, Georgia. She was pastor of chapel services at each assignment.

In 1995, Pastor Roberts reentered the civilian sector and became the founding pastor of Shekina Glory Church in Jesup, Georgia. She served as president for the National Council of Negro Women (Savannah Section), President of the Hinesville Ministerial Alliance, and as a member of numerous organizations and boards. In addition, she conducted workshops and seminars and preached throughout the United States.

In November 1997, Pastor Roberts answered the call to return to active duty military chaplaincy. She was assigned as Chaplain for 702nd Military Intelligence Group and Senior Pastor for Interfaith Worship Service, Fort Gordon, Georgia. She served as the 516th Signal Brigade Chaplain located at Fort Shafter, Hawaii, with unit coverage in Alaska, Mainland Japan and Okinawa. In 2002 she was assigned to Presidio of Monterey as the pastor and chaplain to the cadets and cadre. Later she served as Operations, Plans and Training Chaplain and Associate Pastor for Ord Military Chapel. Pastor Roberts recently became the Garrison Chaplain and Pastor of Selfridge Air National Guard Base Chapel. Her personal military decorations and awards include The Bronze Star, Meritorious Service Medal, Army Service Ribbon and Overseas Service Ribbon.

She and Elisha, her husband of 30 years, have two married children, Elisha Jr. (Verletta), Fort Carson, Colorado and Davola (Arnel), Mount Pleasant, California.